Architecture Apprenticeship Handbook

T0321376

Architecture Apprenticeship Handbook

Daniel Goodricke
Luke Murray

© RIBA Publishing, 2024

Published by RIBA Publishing, 66 Portland Place,
London, W1B 1AD

ISBN 9781915722102

The rights of Daniel Goodricke and Luke Murray to
be identified as the Authors of this Work have been
asserted in accordance with the Copyright, Designs
and Patents Act 1988 sections 77 and 78.

British Library Cataloguing-in-Publication Data
A catalogue record for this book is available from the
British Library.

Commissioning Editor: Alex White
Assistant Editor: Flo Armitage-Hookes
Production: Jane Rogers
Designed and Typeset by Unlimited
Printed and bound by Page Bros, Norwich
Cover images: Hawkins\Brown

While every effort has been made to check the
accuracy and quality of the information given in this
publication, neither the Authors nor the Publisher
accept any responsibility for the subsequent use of
this information, for any errors or omissions that it
may contain, or for any misunderstandings arising
from it.

www.ribapublishing.com

MIX
Paper from
responsible sources
FSC® C023114

Contents

About the authors

The authors are chartered architects and educators, and contributed to the development of architecture degree apprenticeships at two of the largest training providers in the UK. As members of the RIBA Validation Panel and RIBA New Courses Group, both authors are passionate about supporting all pathways to becoming an architect, encouraging excellence and diversity in learner achievement, and ensuring a positive learner experience.

Daniel Goodricke is an Assistant Professor in the Department of Architecture and Built Environment at Northumbria University. He leads the first year of the Architect (Level 7) Degree Apprenticeship, coordinates the End Point Assessment and manages admissions. Daniel is also an external examiner at London South Bank University and the University of Bath, both of which offer architecture apprenticeships.

Luke Murray is Course Leader for the BA (Hons) Architecture course at Ravensbourne University London. During Luke's previous employment, he coordinated both the Level 6 and Level 7 architecture apprenticeships. Luke is also an external examiner to the MArch at De Montfort University, Leicester and an Independent Assessor to the Architect (Level 7) Degree Apprenticeship at the University of Portsmouth.

Dedication

Daniel: To Jessica, for your continuous belief, support and encouragement. To Charlie and Henry, for taking an interest in what I do. And, to my parents, for only ever expecting me to do my best.

Luke: To Rory, for your blazing view of the world and for keeping me on my toes. Fiona, for your generosity and tender support, and Mum, for your selfless benevolence.

Acknowledgements

Daniel: Many thanks to Luke for your quiet diligence, astute advice and passion for opening up the profession – I could not have wished for a better colleague to collaborate with on this publication. Thanks to my colleagues, Paul Jones, Peter Holgate and Kelly Mackinnon, for your professional guidance and friendship. Thanks to fellow members of the RIBA Validation Panel and RIBA New Courses Group for your generosity in sharing your knowledge and experiences.

Luke: A huge thank you to Daniel for your enthusiasm, attentive patience and assiduousness. It has been an absolute pleasure to collaborate on this project with you and I admire your dedication, not only to this handbook but to the profession at large. Thank you to all colleagues who have inspired me and made each day in academia new and exciting, and to Lilly for believing in me from the outset. Thank you to all on the RIBA New Courses Group and Validation Panel; I have learnt so much from you all.

Together: Thanks to academic and industry colleagues, both newly encountered and long-standing, who have contributed to and supported the handbook, including representatives of the Architecture Apprenticeship Forum, as well as Helen Castle, Alex White, Flo Armitage-Hookes, Richard Blackburn and Jane Rogers, reviewers and commenters, apprentices and employers.

Special thanks to the following apprentices and supporting employers, who generously shared their experiences in the form of case studies: Elizabeth Akamo, James Aynsley, Upinder Bahra, Jacinta Barham, Jack Davies, Dorréll Gayle-Menzie, Oliver Howard, Daniel Kinghorn, Eleanor Lee, Mollie Lord, Laura McClorey, Delaram Nabidoost, Sarah Nottet-Madsen, Katie Shannon, Cătălina Stroe, Sudhir Thumbarathy and Santiago Wagner Velez.

And, likewise, a special thanks to those colleagues who contributed their expertise: Andra Antone, Sophie Bailey, Stephanie Beasley-Suffolk, Tim Bell, Dieter Bentley-Gockmann, Harbinder Birdi, Professor Stephen Brookhouse, Richard Collis, Wendy Colvin, Paul Crosby, Dr Susan Dawson, Patrick Devlin, Melissa Dowler, Daniel Dyer, Maria Faraone, Peter Garstecki, Dr Peter Holgate, Simon Howard, Simon Kay-Jones, Matthew Mayes, Kirk McCormack, Marion McCormick, Matthew Morrish, Valentina Moscu, Jane Nicholls, Joanna Parry, Polina Pencheva, Fausto Pereira, Hari Phillips, Neil Pinder, Banah Rashid, Dr Jenny Russell, Mark Siddall, Stephen Smith, Helen Taylor and Ray Verrall.

Foreword

By Dr Jenny Russell
Director of Education and Learning, RIBA

The education of an architect demands not just theoretical knowledge but also hands-on experience. Historically, architects were trained in offices, undertaking the professional exams of the Royal Institute of British Architects in order to join the institute. However, since the Oxford Conference of 1958, which placed an emphasis on learning to realise the intellectual ambitions of architecture, a move from *training* to *education* became the underpinning of that journey of learning.

With the exception of the RIBA Studio model, which maintained the professional examination structure for those working in practice, architectural education has, since that point, been based in higher education, with specific periods in practice. The introduction of the first architecture apprenticeship in 2018 has married together the *training* and *learning* required by an architecture student.

Architecture apprenticeships are not an easy route into the profession. They are complex and heavily regulated. To work successfully they must recognise the critical role of the employer, the educator and the apprentice. On the student's part they require commitment, drive, focus and dedication, in addition to a particularly good relationship with time management. The employer and educator must respect each other's role in the process, recognising not only their place in the education and training of the apprentice, but also their role in guiding them, safe and well, into the profession.

This book successfully takes the complex process of the architecture apprenticeships and breaks it down into digestible and understandable sections, with fantastic real-life examples from those involved in the process. It is more than a useful guide for those involved in apprentices; it is an essential piece of reading for students, employers and educators, and those considering employing an apprentice or setting up a programme. The success of the book makes what is inherently complex seem obvious and straightforward, demystifying the process and opening the possibility of this fantastic route into the profession.

Having known Daniel and Luke for many years, I am not surprised by the care and consideration that has gone into the development and delivery of this handbook. The insights that they bring come from their involvement in the apprenticeship process and their commitment to the profession, architectural education and, in particular, architecture students.

Preface

So, presumably you are considering an architecture apprenticeship?

As a new route into the profession, you are likely to have a lot of questions. Amongst them might be:

- **What is an architecture apprenticeship and is it right for me?**
- **How do I apply and prepare for an apprenticeship?**
- **How can I make the most of my apprenticeship?**
- **How can the apprenticeship support my future career ambitions?**

This handbook answers these questions and more, and aims to demystify the Level 7 apprenticeship. It provides structured guidance and advice for career success and contains information of use to those supporting apprentices on their journey.

The handbook is arranged as follows:

- **Chapter 1** explains what a contemporary architecture apprenticeship is and compares it with other routes into the profession. It will help you to determine whether this route is right for you.

- **Chapter 2** offers advice on finding the 'right employer' and the 'right training provider', guiding you through application processes and procedures involved. It also discusses what can be done if things go wrong.

- **Chapter 3** presents key stages of a typical apprenticeship and indicates what you should expect through your learning. Recognising that no two apprenticeships are alike, it offers insights and illustrated case studies from current and recently qualified apprentices. It also tackles some of the trickier assessments, such as the Design Challenge and Professional Interview en route to qualification.

- **Chapter 4** talks you through the registration processes as an architect. It also presents advanced study options, leading to RIBA accredited specialisms as part of your Continuing Professional Development.

The handbook is interspersed with many training provider and employer contributions, whose expertise and experience of supporting apprentices offer you top tips and practice perspectives, giving you a flavour of what to expect.

As a Level 7 Architecture Apprentice, you will be joining over 600 others who are already benefiting from the reciprocity between academic and workplace learning. Whilst not for everyone, those choosing to pursue this route are considered by industry to be amongst the most sought-after of their generation.

We are especially hopeful that the handbook will encourage those who may not otherwise have continued to professional qualification, not only to succeed but to also become future leaders. We are delighted to be at the start of this journey with you.

The Apprenticeship Journey

Application		

Onboarding	Training Plan	Apprenticeship Agreement	Initial Skills Assessment

Enrolment / Induction	

Training (typically 48 months)	Min. 6 hours per week for off-the-job training	Development of knowledge, skills and behaviours (KSBs) (on-the-job training)
	240 academic credits (Part 2)	Professional experience development record (PEDR)
	Part 3 curriculum	Progress reviews (12 weekly)

GATEWAY	PART 2 AWARD

EPA (6 months)	**Professional Interview** supported by Career Appraisal (15 credits)	**Case Study** supported by Design Challenge (15 credits)
Award	**Part 3** (PGCert, PGDip or Advanced Diploma)	**Apprenticeship Certificate**

Figure 0.1 The Apprenticeship Journey.

Chapter 1
What is an architecture apprenticeship and is it right for me?

This chapter is intended to help you to determine whether an architecture apprenticeship is right for you. It will:

- provide a comprehensive overview of architecture apprenticeships, foregrounded against a very brief history of UK architectural training
- introduce each of the relevant professional, statutory and regulatory stakeholders
- compare architecture apprenticeships to alternative pathways to qualifications.

Architecture apprenticeships

Architecture apprenticeships, as we know them today, were prompted by the introduction of degree apprenticeships incorporating academic qualifications at Level 6 (undergraduate) and Level 7 (postgraduate), as part of the Richard Review of Apprenticeships in 2012,[1] and the subsequent establishment of the Apprenticeship Levy in 2017.[2] They are also professionally recognised by the Architects Registration Board (ARB) and the Royal Institute of British Architects (RIBA).

A contemporary architecture apprenticeship is an integrated degree that combines a job with training to industry standards. It involves a substantial programme of concurrent employer-led ('on-the-job') and university-led ('off-the-job') training, which has been observed by **Patrick Devlin and Marion MacCormick at Pollard Thomas Edwards (PTE),** one of the practices involved in establishing architecture apprenticeships, as 'providing a more balanced body of knowledge than academic or vocational routes can do alone'.[3] Occupational competence is then tested through an independent End Point Assessment (EPA). Apprenticeships represent a remarkable opportunity to undertake the qualifications needed to become an architect without having to leave full-time, paid employment.

Figure 1.1 Liverpool School of Architecture. The first school of architecture to be affiliated with a university and receive validation from the RIBA.

Practice perspective
by Patrick Devlin and Marion MacCormick, Partners, PTE[4]

The principles go back to the first systematic architectural training developed by Sir Christopher Wren in the late seventeenth century, which were then refined up to the establishment of the first UK architectural degree in 1894 at the University of Liverpool. Since the RIBA Oxford Conference in 1958, most architects have qualified via separate, alternating spells in university and practice, and as a result the two strands have not fully complemented and reinforced one another.

Architecture apprenticeships at a glance:

- An alternative path to registration and professional body membership.
- Two levels of study, Level 6 (RIBA Part 1) and Level 7 (Parts 2 and 3).
- Combined professional practical experience and academic teaching.
- Earn while you learn, salaried position with full staff terms and conditions.
- Part-time study in day or block release.
- You do not pay tuition fees, as these are covered by your employer.
- Awarded degree qualifications and professional recognition.

Also consider:

- You will need self-motivation and discipline to balance work and study.
- You will not qualify for any student loans, so you will need to cover your own living costs, including housing, travel and materials.
- Apprentices do not always benefit from the same 'studio culture' as at undergraduate level.

Figure 1.2 Pollard Thomas Edwards, workplace meeting with apprentices. Architecture apprenticeships attribute substantial value to employer-led training.

Architecture Apprenticeship Standard

Each apprenticeship - irrespective of level and discipline - is described as a standard. Standards are developed by a group of employers - referred to as 'trailblazers' - on behalf of the industry and are approved by the Institute for Apprenticeships and Technical Education (IfATE). Each standard comprises:

- an occupational standard - defining competence for an occupation, including required knowledge, skills and behaviours (KSBs)
- an End Point Assessment (EPA) Plan - how occupational competence is assessed and measured

- a funding band allocation – maximum amount available for the off-the-job training (delivered by a training provider).

The Architecture Apprenticeship Standard at Level 7 (hereon in referred to as the standard) is as follows:[5]

- **Occupational Standard:** the KSBs relate to the ARB Criteria for the Prescription of Qualifications at Part 2 and Part 3.[6]
- **End Point Assessment (EPA) Plan:** a Professional Interview supported by a Career Appraisal and a Case Study Report supported by a Design Challenge.[7]
- **Funding Band Allocation:** £21,000 at the time of writing.

Architecture Apprenticeships Trailblazer Group

The Architecture Apprenticeships Trailblazer Group developed the standards for the Architectural Assistant (Level 6) and Architect (Level 7) apprenticeships, following an established process.

Peter Garstecki, Associate Partner and Education Manager at Foster + Partners, reflects on the motivation for their establishment, as well as the process generally, having acted as chair to the Architecture Apprenticeships Trailblazer Group:

Studying architecture under the traditional route is expensive and for some, unaffordable. With the introduction of the Apprenticeship Levy in 2017, Foster + Partners, along with other UK architectural practices, saw an opportunity to collaborate with the ARB and RIBA to form a Trailblazer that would introduce Level 6 and Level 7 standards – a new route to architecture.

Under the apprenticeship proposal the proportion of the practical experience would be increased, the cost of academic education would be paid from the employer's levy pot and apprentices would earn as they learn. This would give access to the profession to those who cannot afford full-time education and diversify routes to register as a UK architect.

The Architecture Apprenticeships Trailblazer Group included:

- Foster + Partners
  Chair
- Lipscomb Jones Architects Ltd[8]
  Architectural Assistant (Level 6) standard sub-lead
- Hawkins\Brown
  Architect (Level 7) standard sub-lead
- Seven Architecture
  Architectural Assistant (Level 6) assessment sub-lead
- Feilden Clegg Bradley Studios (FCBStudios)
  Architectural Assistant (Level 6) assessment sub-lead
- Scott Brownrigg
  Architect (Level 7) assessment sub-lead
- Pollard Thomas Edwards
  *Architecture Apprenticeships Employers' Guide
  sub-lead*
- Allford Hall Monaghan Morris (AHMM)
- Arup
- BDP
- Grimshaw Architects
- HLM Architects
- HOK
- HTA Design LLP
- Perkins&Will
- PLP Architecture
- Purcell
- Ryder Architecture
- Stanton Williams
- tp bennett

Figure 1.3 Foster +
Partners, an early
meeting of the
Architecture
Apprenticeships
Trailblazer Group.
Foster + Partners served
as chair to the group
and hosted several
workshops.

Employers 'need-to-know': What are the benefits of employing an apprentice?

- Future-proof your workforce and address any skills shortages.
- Improve social mobility and diversity within your organisation.
- Improve staff retention and professional development opportunities.
- Bring in new ideas and vision.
- Collaborative opportunities with schools of architecture and other supporting employers.

Routes to register as an architect and professional body membership

The Architecture Apprenticeships Trailblazer Group did not set out to rewrite the route to qualification but rather to provide an alternative to the 'traditional' route within existing ARB, RIBA and IfATE frameworks (see Figure 1.4).

Traditional Route (minimum 7 years)	Year	Apprenticeship Route (minimum 8 years)
Part 1 Study for an undergraduate degree in architecture (BA or BSc).	1 2 3	**Architectural Assistant (Level 6)** Study for an undergraduate degree at university on either a day or block release as part of your apprenticeship. You will work in an architectural practice for the rest of your contracted hours. You will also undertake an End Point Assessment.
Stage 1 Professional Practical Experience ('Year Out') Work for a year in an architectural practice as a Part 1 Architectural Assistant.	4	
Part 2 Study for a Master in Architecture (MArch).	5 6	**Architect Apprenticeship (Level 7)** Study for a Master of Architecture (Part 2) and Advanced Diploma in Professional Practice in Architecture (or equivalent) (Part 3) on either a day or block release as part of your apprenticeship. You will work in an architectural practice for the rest of your contracted hours. You will also undertake an End Point Assessment.
Stage 2 Professional Practical Experience / Part 3 Work full time as a Part 2 Architectural Assistant and study part-time for an Advanced Diploma in Professional Practice in Architecture (or equivalent).	7 8	

Eligible for: Registration as an architect with the Architects Registration Board (ARB); Chartered Membership with the Royal Institute of British Architects (RIBA).

Figure 1.4 Comparison of 'traditional' and apprenticeship routes to registration and professional body membership.

The development of both Architectural Assistant (Level 6) and Architect (Level 7) apprenticeships makes it possible for those wishing to be an apprentice to do so as a school leaver or, as you may be contemplating, to pick up the programme partway through after completing an initial 'traditional' degree at Part 1 (Figure 1.5).

Traditional Route (minimum 7 years)   **Year**   **Apprenticeship Route (minimum 8 years)**

Part 1
Study for an undergraduate degree in architecture (BA or BSc).

1
2
3

Stage 1 Professional Practical Experience ('Year Out')
Work for a year in an architectural practice as a Part 1 Architectural Assistant.

4

5

Architect Apprenticeship (Level 7)
Study for a Master of Architecture (Part 2) and Advanced Diploma in Professional Practice in Architecture (or equivalent) (Part 3) on either a day or block release as part of your apprenticeship. You will work in an architectural practice for the rest of your contracted hours. You will also undertake an End Point Assessment.

6
7
8

Eligible for: Registration as an architect with the Architects Registration Board (ARB); Chartered Membership with the Royal Institute of British Architects (RIBA).

Figure 1.5 Likely route to registration and professional body membership for those already embarked on an architecture career.

Case study Mid-career professional development

James Aynsley completed his Part 1 in 2001 and spent 14 years in professional practice before enrolling on a Level 7 architecture apprenticeship in September 2019 through Northumbria University. He completed his architecture apprenticeship in September 2022 and now works as an Associate. James reflects on his journey in this short interview:

Why did you decide to pursue an architecture apprenticeship?

The creation of the Architect (Level 7) Degree Apprenticeship in 2018 gave me the long-desired opportunity to complete my architectural education whilst maintaining a career. Having worked in practice for many years and, in middle age, assumed many family and work responsibilities, it was no longer practical, or indeed financially viable, for me to return to university on a full-time basis. The combination of off-the-job learning and full-time employment offered by the apprenticeship provided a route to chartership that fully aligned with my personal circumstances.

What were the benefits of undertaking an architecture apprenticeship?

The apprenticeship offered me the chance to fulfil two objectives. The first was to develop, or rather rekindle, my critical design abilities. After working in practice for many years, one develops an architectural shorthand born out of commercial necessity, so I was keen to rediscover a considered and critical approach to design.

Figure 1.6 Northumbria University, James Aynsley, Dementia Care Facility. An illustration for a new dementia care home typology underpinned by primary research and an understanding of the latest innovations in the field of dementia care.

Secondly, I have long felt that, despite my years of experience, I have remained at a disadvantage having not formally studied the RIBA Part 3 curriculum and its emphasis on codes of conduct, practice management, procurement and forms of contract. I felt that a more advanced understanding of such topics was now required.

James was supported by Ryder - a Trailblazer practice and founder of the PlanBEE initiative - which has long promoted alternative routes to qualification to attract a diverse range of people into architecture and the built environment.

Fees, funding and the Apprenticeship Levy

As an apprentice, your employer will cover all training costs, including tuition fees. In a recent national survey,[9] architecture apprentices expressed that this was their principal motive for choosing this route. This is perhaps not surprising, given long-standing concerns about escalating student debts of up to £100,000 for a career path that is increasingly considered to be poor value.[10] Additionally, there is an argument that architecture runs the risk of becoming the preserve of students whose parents can support them through their training.

At the time of writing, the current maximum funding available for the Architect (Level 7) apprenticeship is £21,000 but the total payment required will depend on the Apprenticeship Levy status of your employer. For most architectural practices, this is likely to equate to no more than 5% (or, currently, £262.50 per year). Should a training provider choose to charge fees above this threshold, your employer must cover the additional sum. Please be aware that choosing such a training provider might impact the remuneration that your employer may offer.

It is worth noting that, as an apprentice in full-time employment, you will not have student status and are therefore ineligible for student finance, including a Postgraduate Master's Loan. You will therefore have to budget for expenses such as living costs, field trips, digital and material costs.

Employers 'need-to-know': investing in an apprenticeship

- Architecture apprenticeships at Level 7 are generally low risk, as they represent continued progression to qualification as an architect and may suit existing staff.
- Any contract of employment will need to be at least long enough to allow an apprentice to complete their apprenticeship successfully (four years).
- You will be able to access the government Apprenticeship Levy to either cover the cost of training and accessing an apprentice in full or at 95%.
- The levy is paid direct to the training provider and does not cover the apprentice's salary, so you will need to pay their wages and any other usual employment costs.
- You will need to be able to provide an apprentice with sufficiently complex on-the-job experience to develop the necessary KSBs (including those traditionally associated with Part 3).
- You will need to allow them to combine learning in the workplace with formal training outside the normal working environment (i.e. at university). This may involve day or block release and some flexibility in and around academic deadlines.
- Consider the indirect cost of managing and supporting an apprentice, including administrating the apprenticeship and mentoring and training the apprentice.

Creating a more equitable, diverse and inclusive profession
In recent years there have been concerted efforts to address issues of diversity in architecture education and practice. As examples, Scott Brownrigg has worked with BluePrint for All (formerly the Stephen Lawrence Charitable Trust) to widen participation amongst young people from non-traditional backgrounds. Schools of architecture are also better supporting neurodivergent students to reach their full potential, and local authorities have opened their frameworks so that those designing buildings better reflect those who will be using them.

Educator, activist and founder of HomeGrown Plus,[11] **Neil Pinder,**[12] reflects on the importance of creating a more equitable, diverse and inclusive profession:

The Global Majority [13] is made up by 85% of the world's population. In the UK, it is projected to double to almost 27% of the adult population by 2061. The UK has some of the best cities in the world which are diverse and vibrant. However, the architecture profession does not reflect this diversity. Given all the facts, surely, we should be looking to build programmes which not only nurture and develop the next generation of the Global Majority, but also enables them to achieve great success. Architecture apprenticeships are an excellent way to develop the necessary knowledge and skills for a diverse group of students, which does not leave them with a big financial burden.

Architecture apprenticeships are part of the RIBA's strategy to create a more equitable, diverse and inclusive profession. They have been designed to engage, encourage and inspire creative spatial thinkers from diverse backgrounds, including those of the Global Majority and non-traditional backgrounds.

Figure 1.7 Scott Brownrigg, meeting of apprentices. Apprenticeships encourage the very best spatial thinkers regardless of race, ethnicity or background.

Case study
Widening access

Figure 1.8 Dorréll
Gayle-Menzie (left).

Dorréll Gayle-Menzie comes from a non-traditional background. He studied the International Baccalaureate and Foundation Diploma (Level 3) in Art and Design – as alternatives to A-Levels – en route to an undergraduate degree in architecture. In the two years between graduating and enrolling on a Level 7 architecture apprenticeship, Dorréll contributed to a co-creation scheme in his local neighbourhood and several architectural competitions as part of a platform aimed at helping graduates find roles in architecture practice. Dorréll has always worked in the retail sales sector to support his studies and continues to do so.

What obstacles and hurdles have you encountered in pursuing an architecture career?
Initially, I found it difficult to obtain reliable guidance as neither my school nor family were familiar with the sector. Once studying, I found architecture to be a costly and time-intensive degree. Costs include materials for drawing, model-making and printing, and high-specification laptops,

all of which can impact on the quality of outputs and efficiency. This meant that I needed to work throughout my undergraduate degree to supplement my student maintenance loan. This impacted the time I had available for study, socialising and even sleep. Often, my morning shift ended as one of my lectures started, taking a toll on my work and my stress levels.

How are architecture apprenticeships beginning to alleviate some of these issues and widen access to the profession?
The apprenticeship exposes me to a wealth of knowledge held by colleagues in practice, meaning that I always have guidance on hand. Furthermore, with the apprenticeship being funded by the government, there are no direct costs to me with regards to tuition, and I receive a regular salary and other employee benefits which help with other costs. That said, and for the time being, I continue to work a part-time job on the weekends because of rising living costs. Whilst time pressures are not alleviated - with the apprenticeship demanding time at evenings and weekends - learning is enhanced and expedited.

If you have been inspired by Dorréll's story, why not share your own with Archilogues, a collaborative space where young architects from different academic, professional and socio-economic backgrounds share their experiences and, in turn, inspire others to navigate the industry in their own way.[14]

Architecture apprenticeships may also benefit neurodivergent students. Around one in ten architecture students have disclosed a disability or impairment, the most common being a learning difference such as dyslexia,[15] whilst as many as one in four apprentices are believed to possess a cognitive style that varies from the mainstream. This is perhaps not surprising given the known associations between neurodiversity and creativity, or literally the ability to 'think differently'.

Figure 1.9 Hawkins\ Brown, workshop facilities. Authentic architectural practice, with its emphasis on 'hands-on' learning, is likely to appeal to those with neurodiverse profiles.

Dr Peter Holgate, Associate Professor and Employability Lead in the Department of Architecture and Built Environment at Northumbria University, whose research concerns developing inclusive curricula, including for students with dyslexia,[16] discusses why an apprenticeship might suit those with such learning differences:

Architecture students with dyslexia and similarly neurodiverse profiles can often thrive in practice, despite having struggled with the linguistic focus of normative higher education curricula. The apprenticeship model has substantial potential for synthesising authentic architectural practice with an individuated focus on apprentices' visual-spatial and interpersonal intelligences.

For architectural practices and the wider industry, there exists an exciting opportunity to:

- open itself up to the best and most diverse talent available
- benefit from untapped knowledge, experiences and skills
- promote innovation
- access other projects, communities and markets
- better reflect and serve society as a whole.

A very brief history of UK architectural training
by Ray Verrall

Associate Lecturer and PhD candidate at Newcastle University's School of Architecture, Planning and Landscape, Ray Verrall, whose research explores the values and tensions surrounding the RIBA's 1958 Oxford Conference on architectural education, explains:

Contemporary debates about architectural training and education remain rooted in historical questions of vocational identity and purpose. What is an architect? What skills are required for practice, and how are they best acquired?

Most intending architects in the eighteenth century trained through a combination of apprenticeship and private study, with pupillage becoming the dominant mode by the end of the century.[17] A good pupillage could lead to a successful career, but the system was both unregulated and unreliable. Partly in response, a series of small architectural societies initiated a project of professionalisation to improve training standards and distinguish architectural practice from other industry actors. This led to the founding of the RIBA in the 1830s, and the eventual passing of the Architects (Registration) Acts a century later, restricting entry to the profession by examination and legislation.[18]

This sequence of events had been prolonged by decades of fierce debate about whether architecture was a profession or an art – a dangerously misleading dichotomy that polarised architectural educators at the start of the twentieth century. Contention centred around the question of 'the right environment' for the production of architects, and the relationship between training and education.[19] Resistance to professionalisation was led by architects associated with the Art Workers' Guild, who viewed their vocation as a creative activity best learned in practice through experiential understanding of building materials and processes. Support came predominantly from Neoclassicists who emphasised managerial aspects of practice and favoured a theory-driven approach to

Figure 1.10 (opposite) Kirk McCormack (adapted). The Histomap. Four Hundred Years of Architectural Education: Relative Power of Routes to Qualification as an Architect through Time.

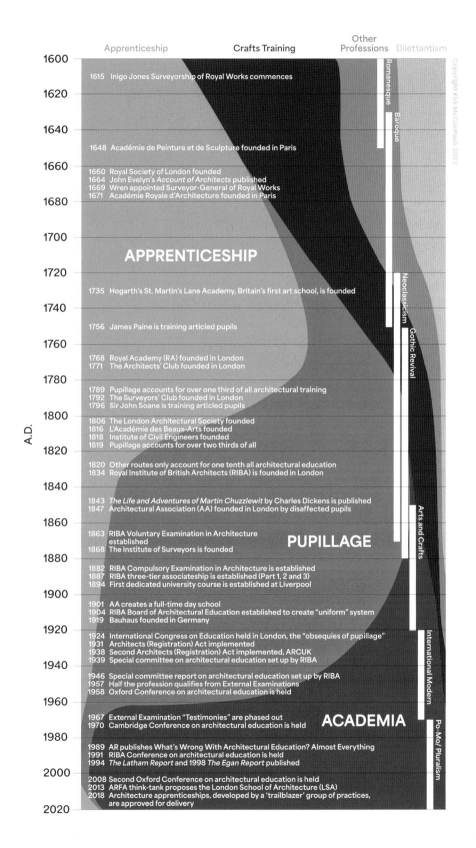

Apprenticeship   Crafts Training   Other Professions   Dilettantism

A.D.

1600

1615   Inigo Jones Surveyorship of Royal Works commences

1620

1640

1648   Académie de Peinture et de Sculpture founded in Paris

1660

1660   Royal Society of London founded
1664   John Evelyn's *Account of Architects* published
1669   Wren appointed Surveyor-General of Royal Works
1671   Académie Royale d'Architecture founded in Paris

1680

1700

APPRENTICESHIP

1720

1735   Hogarth's St. Martin's Lane Academy, Britain's first art school, is founded

1740

1756   James Paine is training articled pupils

1760

1768   Royal Academy (RA) founded in London
1771   The Architects' Club founded in London

1780

1789   Pupillage accounts for over one third of all architectural training
1792   The Surveyors' Club founded in London
1796   Sir John Soane is training articled pupils

1800

1806   The London Architectural Society founded
1816   L'Académie des Beaux-Arts founded
1818   Institute of Civil Engineers founded
1819   Pupillage accounts for over two thirds of all

1820

1820   Other routes only account for one tenth all architectural education
1834   Royal Institute of British Architects (RIBA) is founded in London

1840

1843   *The Life and Adventures of Martin Chuzzlewit* by Charles Dickens is published
1847   Architectural Association (AA) founded in London by disaffected pupils

1860

1863   RIBA Voluntary Examination in Architecture established
1868   The Institute of Surveyors is founded

PUPILLAGE

1880

1882   RIBA Compulsory Examination in Architecture is established
1887   RIBA three-tier associateship is established (Part 1, 2 and 3)
1894   First dedicated university course is established at Liverpool

1900

1901   AA creates a full-time day school
1904   RIBA Board of Architectural Education established to create "uniform" system
1919   Bauhaus founded in Germany

1920

1924   International Congress on Education held in London, the "obsequies of pupillage"
1931   Architects (Registration) Act implemented
1938   Second Architects (Registration) Act implemented, ARCUK
1939   Special committee on architectural education set up by RIBA

1940

1946   Special committee report on architectural education set up by RIBA
1957   Half the profession qualifies from External Examinations
1958   Oxford Conference on architectural education is held

1960

1967   External Examination "Testimonies" are phased out
1970   Cambridge Conference on architectural education is held

ACADEMIA

1980

1989   AR publishes What's Wrong With Architectural Education? Almost Everything
1991   RIBA Conference on architectural education is held
1994   *The Latham Report* and 1998 *The Egan Report* published

2000

2008   Second Oxford Conference on architectural education is held
2013   ARFA think-tank proposes the London School of Architecture (LSA)
2018   Architecture apprenticeships, developed by a 'trailblazer' group of practices, are approved for delivery

2020

Romanesque
Baroque
Neoclassicism
Gothic Revival
Arts and Crafts
International Modern
Po-Mo/Pluralism

education based upon the Beaux-Arts-inspired American model of full-time academic courses.

Despite a rapid increase in the number of full-time courses available (many 'recognised' and promoted by the RIBA's new Board of Architectural Education), various forms of apprenticeship combined with part-time study remained popular with both students and employers throughout the first half of the twentieth century. This all changed when the RIBA's 1958 Oxford Conference determined that future architects should be educated exclusively at university-level institutions through full-time recognised courses, with minimal periods of office-based training.[20] The balance had shifted. Architecture was arguably no longer a vocation, but through professionalisation it had become an intellectual discipline.[21]

Professional, statutory and regulatory frameworks

Now that you have a good knowledge of architecture apprenticeships, this section will introduce you to each of the professional, statutory and regulatory stakeholders. You have already been introduced to one, the Architecture Apprenticeships Trailblazer Group, and will likely be familiar with the RIBA and ARB, but there are several others that you should know about at the outset of your apprenticeship. Many of the stakeholders have directly contributed to this section, wishing to explain why architecture apprenticeships are important and how they aim to support you on your apprenticeship journey.

Responsible body	Role
Architecture Apprenticeships Trailblazer Group (led by Foster + Partners)	Development and review of architecture standards, promotion of architecture apprenticeships
Institute for Apprenticeships and Technical Education (IfATE)	Apprenticeship standards development, review and approval
Architects Registration Board (ARB)	Prescription of architecture apprenticeships
Royal Institute of British Architects (RIBA)	Validation of architecture apprenticeships
Office for Standards in Education, Children's Services and Skills (Ofsted)	Inspection and assessment of training provision
Education and Skills Funding Agency (ESFA) acting on behalf of Department for Education (DfE)	Apprenticeship funding, value for money and financial health and sustainability of training providers
Office for Students (OfS)	Standards of higher-education qualifications awarded by degree-awarding bodies

Table 1.1 Roles and responsibilities of organisations involved in architecture apprenticeships.

Institute for Apprenticeships and Technical Education (IfATE)

IfATE works with employers to develop, approve, review and revise apprenticeships and technical qualifications. It worked closely with the Architecture Apprenticeships Trailblazer Group in 2017-18 to develop and approve the Architectural Assistant (Level 6) and Architect (Level 7) Occupational Standards.

Jill Nicholls, Head of Construction and the Built Environment, Transport and Logistics at IfATE, expands on its role in support of apprentice learning:

IfATE puts employers in charge of designing training programmes, because they understand best how to fill the skills gaps in the economy and prepare apprentices for long and successful careers.

The government agency supports hundreds of employers in the architecture profession, of all shapes and sizes from across the country, to identify the KSBs you must learn to become occupationally competent architects. IfATE also helps employers design the assessment you will need to pass at the end of your apprenticeship to prove you really know how to do the given job.

IfATE takes a collaborative approach to the review and, where necessary revision, of standards to ensure that your training is fit for purpose and enables you to address existing and future challenges facing the profession.

Architects Registration Board (ARB)

As the professional regulator,[22] the ARB is responsible for setting the standards for registration as an architect. It fulfils this role by setting criteria and processes that institutions teaching architecture must meet in order for their students to qualify and register as architects.[23]

There is no difference in the requirements to register for graduates of an apprenticeship as opposed to those who graduate with 'traditional' qualifications. The same is true in terms of professional practical experience.

If you are contemplating practising within the European Union, it is worth noting that prescribed apprenticeships comply with the requirement of Mutual Recognition of Professional Qualifications Directive (2006/36/EC) and are notified for listing under Annex V of the Directive.

Simon Howard, Director of Standards at the ARB, discusses forthcoming changes to architectural education and how apprenticeships are already contributing to this agenda:

We are changing the way we educate and train architects in the UK, by developing a regulatory model that focuses on the outcomes required of an individual at the end of their initial period of education and training.

We believe that the most important factor is what a newly qualified architect should be able to do – not how they got there. This means that we are open to considering different routes to registration, particularly those which might widen access to the profession. Apprenticeships are a key opportunity in this regard and we are already seeing success on this route.

Royal Institute of British Architects (RIBA)

The RIBA is responsible for the validation of architecture apprenticeships. As most apprenticeships are offered as pathways within existing programmes, they will likely be immediately validated and considered for continued validation alongside all other validated programmes at the providers' next five-yearly visit.[24] As architecture apprenticeships last a minimum of four academic years, it is likely that you will encounter an RIBA visiting board. Your reflections on teaching and learning, workload management, online and offline facilities and links to practice will inform the student course appraisal and student meeting, and your academic work may be selected to feature in the exhibition or portfolio sample.

As an apprentice, you are eligible to apply for RIBA student membership and select scholarships and bursaries, and be nominated for RIBA Student Awards and President's Medals. You can also access free extra learning content via

Figure 1.11 RIBA President's Medals Student Awards 2023. Members of the RIBA Education and Learning team reviewing nominated entries from schools of architecture internationally.

RIBA Academy and add your voice to big issues like diversity and inclusion in architecture and the climate emergency.

Joanna Parry, Head of Professional Education at the RIBA, discusses the importance of architecture apprenticeships to the institute, profession and wider public:

The RIBA was delighted to support the Trailblazer practices in developing architecture apprenticeships, seeing their potential to attract new talent to consider a career in architecture and enable practices to offer enhanced staff development. Apprenticeships represent a significant step towards a more socially inclusive architectural profession, as one of several flexible training routes available to students.

With a quarter of all UK schools of architecture delivering apprenticeship pathways which meet the RIBA's validation requirements at Parts 1, 2 and 3, apprentices are completing their qualifications and becoming Chartered Architects; a proud moment for us.

The RIBA will continue to work with stakeholders to drive forward apprenticeships in the future.

The RIBA has recently implemented a new Education and Professional Development Framework, comprising Themes and Values for Architectural Education, aimed at ensuring that architects, architecture students and apprentices possess the knowledge, skills and experience required to respond to the challenges facing our world, society and profession.[25]

Office for Standards in Education, Children's Services and Skills (Ofsted)
You will likely have heard of Ofsted from your time in compulsory schooling. In recent years, Ofsted assumed responsibility for the inspection of higher and degree apprenticeships in addition to those at lower levels.

You can access published outcomes and reports from both monitoring visits and full inspections to any training provider on the Ofsted website.[26] These reports make judgments against three criteria, rating each as either outstanding, good, requires improvement or inadequate:

1. Overall effectiveness.
2. The quality of education and training.
3. Leadership and management.

There is much terminology associated with apprenticeships that are unfamiliar to higher education settings and therefore have the potential to cause some confusion. At this stage of your apprenticeship journey, it is worth being aware of two: safeguarding and fundamental British values.

1. What is safeguarding and how does it relate to apprenticeships?
Safeguarding is the action taken to promote the welfare of children and young people and to protect them from harm. Key safeguarding mechanisms available to apprentices are likely to include central university resources, pastoral tutoring and review meetings with your coach and workplace mentor.

2. What are fundamental British values and how can you give evidence of them?

Fundamental British values	Examples
Democracy	Equality of opportunity to select and develop design project and research themes; parity of learning experience irrespective of location and circumstances
The rule of law	Knowledge of UK legal system, civil liabilities and the laws of contract and tort
Individual liberty	Self-direction of individual apprentices to pursue their own interests, specialisms and shape their own career paths
Mutual respect	Professional courtesies within academia and practice; The Architects Code: Standard 12 Respect for others
Tolerance	Encouraging and supporting diversity in the profession

During an Ofsted visit, an inspector may wish to speak to you. If so, they are likely to do this either during a facilitated session, teaching session, progress review meeting or by giving you a phone call.

Table 1.2 Five fundamental British values. Examples of how you can give evidence of them.[27]

Susan Dawson, Consultant Ofsted Expert with architecture-subject specialism, answers the question, 'How can I contribute to an Ofsted inspection?':

- **Progress:** Be prepared to discuss the progress you are making against the KSBs of the standard, and the impact of the apprenticeship on you since your start date. It might be useful to think of it as: What is it that you are able to do now that you were not able to do before?

- **Feedback:** Consider the feedback you have been given from your lecturers and work colleagues, and its impact on your performance both in the workplace and at university. How has the feedback enabled you to continue to develop?
- **Fundamental British values:** Be aware of fundamental British values and how these are significant in an architectural context. Are you able to share examples of how your apprenticeship has developed your ability to engage, debate and challenge for the benefit of wider society and in accordance with British values? (See Table 1.2).
- **Safeguarding:** Consider if you feel safe in the workplace, on site, on campus and online. Are you able to maintain a reasonable work-study-life balance and manage stress? If not, would you know how to get advice and support?
- **Career progression:** Share examples of how you have been supported to progress. This may be support around changing employers, project experience or even promotion.
- **What is next?:** Have a clear line of sight to what is next. This may be the End Point Assessment or further career progression. This should be outlined in your individual Training Plan.
- **Final advice:** Relax, be open and honest. Inspections are to celebrate the good and to identify areas which may need additional focus for improvement. The inspection is not to catch you out!

Education and Skills Funding Agency (ESFA)

The ESFA – an executive agency sponsored by the Department for Education – is responsible for ensuring that public funding for the delivery of apprenticeships is appropriately spent. It principally checks that funding is spent on training that fits the apprenticeship model, and fulfils learner needs and meets quality regulations. It conducts periodic audits of training providers to ensure compliance with what is a complex set of apprenticeship funding rules.

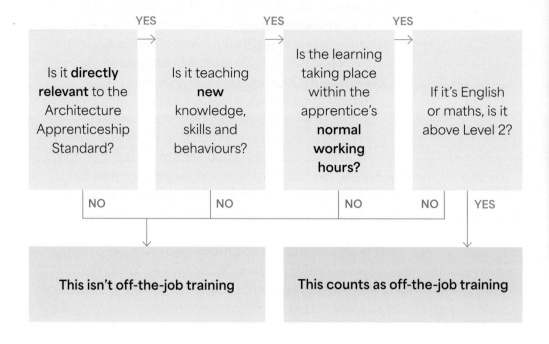

Figure 1.12 Steps to determining whether an activity counts as off-the-job training.

Whilst much of this will be the concern of your training provider, you need to know a couple of points about the ESFA and its apprenticeship funding rules:

1. Funding cannot be used to deliver learning that you already know. You will therefore be asked to complete an Initial Skills Assessment (ISA), mapping your existing KSBs against those of the standard.[28]
2. You should receive a minimum of six hours per week off-the-job training if you are a full-time apprentice (working at least 30 hours per week). You will need to properly record, evidence and track this.

Some apprentices and employers have initially found it difficult to determine whether an activity counts as off-the-job training. Figure 1.13, based on guidance provided by IfATE, may help you and your employer design suitable training activities.

It is true that most off-the-job training comprises university-led academic study, including studio projects, taught modules, Virtual Learning Environment (VLE) engagement and self-directed study. There is generally a need to supplement this with training in the workplace or at an external location during non-term-time. Common employer-led off-the-job training activities include shadowing senior colleagues, Continuing Professional Development (CPD) and new software training.

Top tip for off-the-job training activities

Depending on your existing experience, less commonly performed tasks such as site inspections, post-occupancy evaluations, access audits and Construction Design and Management (CDM) activities may also be counted.

It is worth noting that time spent on initial assessment, onboarding, progress reviews, on-programme assessments and, where applicable, English and maths up to Level 2 does not count towards off-the-job training.

Office for Students (OfS)

OfS is the independent regulator of higher education in England and acts as the External Quality Assurance (EQA) provider to all integrated degree apprenticeships.[29] OfS ensures the quality, relevance and reliability of the End Point Assessment (EPA). It is intended to provide you with the confidence that you have been assessed fairly, and contributes to the credibility of apprenticeships amongst employers, although professional recognition will likely better serve these purposes.

Comparison of architecture apprenticeship to alternative pathways to qualification

Whilst routes to becoming an architect are arguably not as varied as they once were – as illustrated in the histomap infographic featured on page 19 – there still exist several postgraduate options for you to consider.

Table 1.3 compares Part 2 programmes across a range of factors, from duration to cost – arguably the most differentiating – and from expected academic workload to available support network:[30]

	Apprenticeship	Full time
Duration	4 years	2 years
Cost	No cost to apprentice	£18,500 (£9,250 / year)
Eligible for student finance	No	Yes
Where are you based?	Near workplace (in England)	Living in or near university
Entry requirements	Successful completion of Part 1 with a minimum grade; eligible to join an apprenticeship scheme	Usually, successful completion of Part 1; portfolio; interview; English proficiency (at least IELTS 6.5)
Programme co-requirements	Employment in a relevant role (typically as an Architectural Assistant) and have appropriate employer support; Level 2 (equivalent to GCSE A*-C or 9-4) in maths and English by the End Point Assessment gateway (latest)	None
Expected academic workload	Equivalent of two to three days per week	30 hours / week

Table 1.3 Comparison
of current Part 2 programmes.

Part time	Practice-complemented (hybrid)	RIBA Studio Diploma
3 years	2 years	Min. 3 years, max. 9 years
£18,500 (£6,167 / year)	£18,500 (£9,250 / year)	£9,375 plus personal (academic) tutor fees (approx. £3,600) (£4,325 / year, based on three year duration)
Yes	Yes	No
Living near university	Near workplace but with access to course provider	UK, European Economic Area (EEA), Isle of Man, Channel Islands and Switzerland
Successful completion of Part 1 with a minimum grade	Successful completion of Part 1 with a minimum grade	Successful completion of Part 1; portfolio; online interview; English proficiency (at least IELTS 6.5)
None	Confirmation of a placement with a partner practice	Full-time, permanent employment (> 24 hours / week) under the supervision of an office mentor (an architect who is registered in the country you work in)
20 hours / week, on average	30 hours / week	10-12 hours / week across the full 12-month calendar year

	Apprenticeship	Full time
Contact time at university	1 day / week during term-time	2 days / week
Integrated practice-based component	Yes	No
Support network	Subject-specific academic tutors; pastoral tutor; workplace mentor; PEDR (professional experience development record) mentor; university-assigned apprentice coach	Subject-specific academic tutors; pastoral tutor
Freedom to move between practices	Yes (subject to employer eligibility and ESFA funding rules)	N/A
Outcome	Master of Architecture (MArch) or Master of Studies (MSt); Part 2 qualification; Advanced Diploma in Professional Practice in Architecture (or equivalent), Part 3 qualification; Apprenticeship Certificate	Master of Architecture (MArch) (or equivalent); Part 2 qualification
Part 3 (only relevant during or after Part 2)	Integrated into four-year apprenticeship completion of Part 2 (subject to PEDR completion)	Min. 24 months (inc. 12 months post-Part 2) professional practical experience required prior to enrolment

Table 1.3 (continued).

Part time	Practice-complemented (hybrid)	RIBA Studio Diploma
2 days / week	3–4 days / week in practice, 1–2 days / week at university (and vice versa)	Up to eight times per year and meetings with personal (academic) tutor every 2–3 weeks
No	Yes	Yes
Subject-specific academic tutors; pastoral tutor	Subject-specific academic tutors; pastoral tutor; workplace colleagues	Office mentor, personal (academic) tutor and peer support network
N/A	Yes	Yes
Master of Architecture (MArch) (or equivalent); Part 2 qualification	Master of Architecture (MArch) (or equivalent); Part 2 qualification	Part 2 qualification
Option to immediately enrol following completion of Part 2 (subject to PEDR completion)	Min. 24 months (inc. 12 months post-Part 2) professional practical experience required prior to enrolment	Option to either immediately enrol following completion of Part 2 (subject to PEDR completion) or, in exceptional cases, concurrent to final year

The apprenticeship and RIBA Studio routes should be considered carefully. Applicants who believe these to be quick and easy ways to qualify are likely to be ill-prepared for the degree of commitment demanded; both require high levels of self-discipline and time-management skills.

Full time

Whilst you may not be considering studying full time, it remains by far the most popular choice of students entering RIBA validated Part 2 courses.[31] Full-time options conclude in less time but cost more and afford the largest choice in terms of schools and location. This route has several potential benefits, including:

- more time and space for theoretical inquiry, experimentation and time-intensive activities like physical model-making
- a greater sense of 'studio culture'
- a more rounded 'university experience'.

They are also more likely to help you achieve a reasonable study-life balance.

Most training providers will allow you to transfer to the full-time equivalent course, should you decide midway through your apprenticeship that it is not the right study mode for you. It can also act as a fail-safe should you be made redundant and not succeed in finding alternative employment.

Part time

With apprenticeships now making up the majority of those studying RIBA validated Part 2 courses on a part-time basis,[32] fewer schools of architecture are offering a part-time provision. If you are interested in studying on a part-time basis, you are encouraged to speak to individual schools of architecture and ask whether they can accommodate this. Remember that you will be liable for tuition fees, albeit on a pro-rata basis, but you will likely qualify for a Postgraduate Master's Loan to help with course fees and living costs.[33] You will presumably choose to work alongside your part-time studies, but this need not be in a relevant position.

Practice-complemented (hybrid)

As a relatively recent initiative, some schools of architecture are recognising practice-based learning against academic credits to a full-time course – a sort of hybrid. We have chosen to refer to these as 'practice-complemented' although other terms are also commonly used, such as 'practice-based' or 'distance-learning' programmes. This typically takes place in the first year, with students being predominantly based in architectural practice whilst undertaking a combination of practice-based and academic work. You will be expected to find a suitable placement – your employer during your 'year out' would be an obvious choice – however, this experience will not count in terms of your minimum 24 months of professional practice experience. The second year reverts to a more normative mode of study, with a design thesis and dissertation demanding your focus.

The Welsh School of Architecture at Cardiff University and Loughborough University (if opting for the Practice Pathway) offer such courses, yet, arguably the most innovative and ambitious is that delivered by the London School of Architecture (LSA).

Case study
The London School of Architecture (LSA)

The London School of Architecture, founded in 2015 and known as the LSA, is a small, independent school of architecture based in east London and the first since the establishment of the Architectural Association in 1847.

The LSA emerged from the Alternative Routes for Architecture think-tank, launched in *The Architectural Review*, which sought to tackle a growing crisis in the funding of architectural education.[34] The school was established with a clear vision that people living in cities should experience more fulfilled and more sustainable lives. Its mission is to build architectural programmes and learning experiences that are affordable and accessible.[35]

The LSA operates on a reduced fee basis, where tuition fees are balanced with placement salaries.[36] During the first year of the full-time programme – known as the Inter-Practice Year – you would spend three days a week on a Student Placement facilitated by the LSA's London-based Practice Network and the remaining two days a week on academic projects, before undertaking a thesis in your final year.

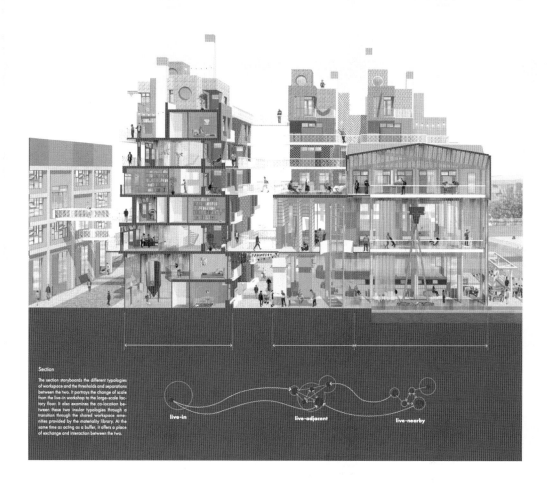

Section

The section storyboards the different typologies of workspace and the thresholds and separations between the two. It portrays the change of scale from the live-in workshop to the large-scale factory floor. It also examines the co-location between these two insular typologies through a transition through the shared workspace amenities provided by the materiality library. At the same time as acting as a buffer, it offers a place of exchange and interaction between the two.

live-in   live-adjacent   live-nearby

Figure 1.13 LSA, Yavor Ivanov, The Live Work City. An examination of new models for co-locating living and working in the city in the context of shifting lifestyles and work patterns.

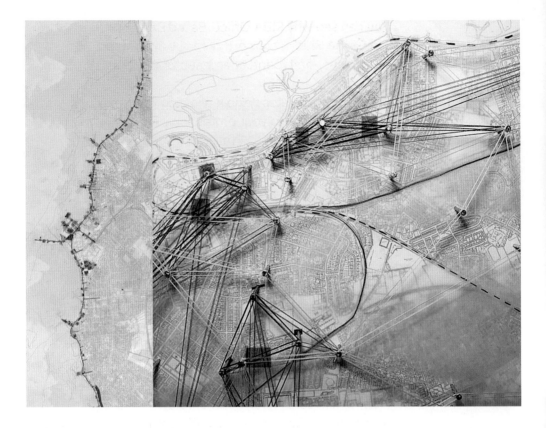

RIBA Studio Diploma

If you wish to continue working full time in practice,[37] retain your salary and gain your Part 2 qualification, another option is to enrol as an office-based student on the RIBA Studio Diploma in partnership with the School of Architecture at Oxford Brookes University.

It is not a taught course and therefore, in comparison with an apprenticeship, the role of your office mentor and chosen personal tutor[38] is arguably of heightened importance as between you, and within a provided framework, you will devise your architectural education. They will:

- support you in developing your understanding of architectural design and practice, including inquiry and skills beyond your immediate office experience
- tutor you on your design projects and dissertation
- assist in the preparation of personal (academic) and practice-based portfolios.

Figure 1.14 RIBA Studio Diploma, Laura Goodrick, Promenade University. A masterplan study into how coastal academic institutions have the ability to transform the socio-economic societies in which they are located.

You can see why RIBA Office-Based Examination (now RIBA Studio) alumni Kirk McCormack likens it to a 'twenty-first- century architectural pupillage'.[39]

The course operates flexibly, allowing you to study at a pace relative to your professional and personal circumstances. This is formally managed through a combination of Annual Learning Contracts and Statements of Academic Intent. The flexibilities include expanding the study period of each year, multiple submission dates without penalty and, if necessary, the ability to take a year out. **Dr Maria Faraone, RIBA Studio Programme Director,** explains that 'every opportunity to support the high-pressure life circumstances of students in practice, including the awarding of credit to the learning that takes place in practice, helped shape this programme'.

This route, originally conceived as a social betterment programme, has proved especially popular with those working at a senior level within professional practice who cannot afford to free up sufficient time to study part time, and those who work and live in remote geographical locations, as mandatory in-person attendance at Oxford Brookes University is kept to a minimum. Over the past few years, it has increasingly become a viable option for students who could attend full-time education but are finding practice-based routes more viable, and is therefore strongly aligned with the full-time Part 2 course.

Is an architecture apprenticeship right for me?
Whilst only you can answer this question, it can be useful to hear from existing cohorts of architecture apprentices. In response to a recent national survey,[40] 88% of apprentices stated that they would recommend the route, and reflected on both the opportunities and unforeseen challenges of an architecture apprenticeship.

The five most common opportunities were:

1. Financial security of retained employment, paid tuition fees and avoidance of further student debt.

2. Potential reciprocity between workplace and academic learning,[41] and simultaneous access to educational and technical resources.
3. Preference for on-the-job (or hands-on) learning.
4. Real-world experience, exposure and network of professional practice.
5. Supported learning and career pathway.

The five most common unforeseen challenges were:[42]

1. Difficulty maintaining reasonable work-study-life balance, with some apprentices citing mental health issues and burnout; apprentices can easily fall behind.
2. Reluctance amongst some employers to negotiate remuneration.
3. Additional administration associated with apprenticeships generally (e.g. logging of off-the-job training activities, progress reviews, etc.).
4. Changing personal and family circumstances.
5. Difficulty meeting the off-the-job requirement outside of term-time.

Practice perspective
by Patrick Devlin and Marion MacCormick, Partners, PTE[43]

It is clear that those successfully completing the Level 7 apprenticeship have a high order of design and practical ability, as well as no increase in their student debt. Successful completion of Level 7 apprenticeship takes hard work by the apprentice, good levels of communication from the university, and good working opportunities and responsive support from the employer. It suits students with high levels of natural ability who are prepared to put in the additional hours that will sometimes be needed. If these criteria are met, successful apprentices look very likely to be among the most sought-after architects of their generation.

2

Chapter 2
How do I apply and prepare for an apprenticeship?

This chapter will discuss how to apply and prepare for an architecture apprenticeship. It:

- contains advice on looking for the right employer and training provider
- provides guidance for collating a curriculum vitae (CV) and portfolio
- introduces the purpose of the Initial Skills Assessment and Training Plan
- outlines support available to you.

Applying for a job is not easy, particularly if you have not yet had any professional experience to demonstrate your competences. Without any experience, how do you then apply for a role as a Part 1 Architectural Assistant? And how do you simultaneously obtain commitment from an employer to sponsor the continuation of your education, whilst offering a full-time salary at the National Living Wage?[1] How do you obtain approval to spend, on average, one day per week out of the office and to have a workplace mentor to support your learning? To make such a request as a long-standing employee is difficult, but for a new employee it can be even more daunting.

Yet, with the inception of architecture apprenticeships, it has become possible to achieve all of the above when following the right steps to demonstrate your dedication to a career in the profession. And this chapter will help demystify these steps for you.

If you are currently completing your initial year of professional practical training as a Part 1 Architectural Assistant, then this

Figure 2.1 (opposite) Flow diagram presenting the possible routes to an architecture apprenticeship.

Are you over 16, living in England, and not in full-time education?

NO → To be eligible for an apprenticeship in England, you must first meet these three key criteria, set by the UK Government

YES

Have you completed undergraduate education and received ARB/RIBA Part 1 or equivalent?

NO → To enrol on the L7 architecture apprenticeship, you need to complete your Part 1 or equivalent. Schools offering Part 1 can be found on arb.org.uk

YES

Are you able to balance university and practice work, working independently and as part of a team?

NO → You may be better suited to study full or part time. You can find all validated architecture schools at www.architecture.com

YES

Do you have any other commitment that may impact an apprenticeship?

YES

NO

Are you keen to explore collaborative opportunities through university and practice?

NO → Do you enjoy the university environment as a space for learning and networking?

YES → Although apprentices receive access to all the same resources and facilities as all other students, as a full-time student, you will have more time to explore and use these facilities

YES

NO

Are you currently employed in architectural practice in England?

NO → To study on an architecture apprenticeship, you need an offer of employment in England. You can search for opportunities at jobs.architecture.com

YES

Is there a qualified architect in your company willing to be your mentor?

YES

Is your employer able/willing to sponsor your apprenticeship?

NO → If your employer cannot support your studies or you cannot meet the Knowledge, Skills and Behaviours at your practice, you will need to find a new employer to continue your journey.

YES

Are you paid for your work, will you be offered time to study and have access to a mentor?

NO → Your employer should agree to pay at least the National Living Wage, following RIBA recommendations, offer you a mentor and allow you time to be in university

YES

At this point, you meet all the initial requirements to pursue an architecture apprenticeship. Continue reading to find out the next steps in your journey.

is a great time to start thinking about the next steps in your career. If you are considering the architecture apprenticeship, then an initial conversation with your employer is highly recommended, as you need their support – both in terms of time and resources – from the outset. To start this process, you need the most up-to-date information on architecture apprenticeships and to understand the responsibilities of both parties. If you are not currently working as a Part 1 Architectural Assistant, you will first need to obtain an offer of employment before you can embark on an apprenticeship.

This chapter will help you to prepare for your apprenticeship and it provides information on key areas to think about when planning for it. It outlines key stakeholders and their roles, and offers suggestions to support the applications you make. It will also discuss ways to find an appropriate employer and training provider for your needs, as well as outlining the apprenticeship application process. Whatever you decide to be the best approach for you, this chapter will offer the knowledge to make informed decisions about your career path in architecture.

Looking for the right employer and training provider

There are multiple reasons why an architecture apprenticeship may appeal over and above traditional architectural education routes, so think carefully about what the benefits are for you.

Once you have decided to enrol on an architecture apprenticeship, the first step is to ensure you have an employer willing to sponsor you. To be eligible, you must be in full-time employment in a company that is able to ensure that you can meet the KSBs of the standard. With such a diverse range of practice types, sizes and locations, there is unfortunately no one-size-fits-all approach to finding the right employer to suit you. In order to be eligible, you must be living in England and ensure that your employer is in England and that they can offer you work on projects in England for a minimum of 50% of your time. This is a significant government criterion and aligns with Ofsted's *Strategic Priorities (2022)*[2] to improve lives and raise education standards in England, so is a determining factor when researching employers. Below are four areas that might help when looking for the right employer.

1. Logistical considerations

These items are about time, energy and resources, related to your day-to-day activities. A few key considerations are:

- **Office location and travel**
  - Is it feasible for me to travel to the office Monday to Friday?
  - How long will the journey take?
  - How will I get to and from the office?
  - Can I travel by train, bus, car, bike or foot?
- **Working hours**
  - How long will my day be?
- **Working from home**
  - Is there a work-from-home policy? Many practices now have policies to support diverse work patterns and needs.
  - How does the practice's approach suit my individual working pattern and apprenticeship?
- **Training**
  - Are there any training requirements for the role?
  - What training might I need to complete?
  - How close is the office to prospective training providers?

2. Economic and other benefit considerations

It is important to consider your salary and outgoings to assess financial viability. Employers can offer different salaries, which will be determined by numerous factors such as practice size, location, income and overheads.

It is highly recommended that you consider the following points and questions to ask:

- **Salary**
  - What will my salary be? Is it negotiable?
  - Will it cover the costs of living expenses, including travel, accommodation, utilities, food, study materials and personal expenses?
  - Will I be paid weekly or monthly?

- **Opportunities for professional development**
  - Is there potential for promotion and greater responsibility?
  - What are the different role hierarchies?
  - How long does progression typically take within the practice?
  - Can I become a shareholder (employee-ownership or Share Incentive Plans – SIPs)?
- **Employee benefits**
  - Are there any health and wellbeing benefits, such as gym membership, physiotherapy or access to assistance programmes (Employee Assistance Programme – EAP)
  - What is the employer's pension scheme?
  - Do they offer an employee referral bonus?
  - Is there an annual bonus for meeting performance targets?
  - Is there any employee recognition bonus?
- **Annual leave**
  - What is my initial annual leave entitlement?
  - Does it increase with length of service?
  - Do they allow flexitime and/or time off in lieu (TOIL)?
  - What is the maternity/paternity leave policy?
- **Study leave allowance**
  - Can I take days off to focus on studies at critical points in the academic year?

3. Practical considerations

Regarding the office environment and projects, it is good to think about current gaps in your knowledge and how an employer might support with this:

- **Size of the office**
  - Is it a micro-practice with up to five employees or an international team with global offices across different locations?
  - Does everyone have their own desk or hot desk?
  - Are there meeting rooms, crit spaces and breakout spaces?
  - Are there good kitchen facilities or a cafeteria?

- **Types of projects**
  - Is there a defined sector or specialism?
  - Does the employer work for select clients only?
  - What is the typical size and complexity of the projects?
  - Are these competitions, one-off houses, complex residential, public- or mixed-use?
- **RIBA Work Stages**[3]
  - What stages (0–7) am I likely to be working on?
- **Mentorship**
  - Who will be my mentor and how closely will I be working with them?
  - Will I work with my mentor on a daily or weekly basis?
- **Office environment**
  - What type of office environment would I like to work in?
  - Does the space suit my preferences?

Figure 2.2 Elliott Architects, office interior. A small employer in Northumberland with a track record of supporting apprentices to qualification.

Employers 'need-to-know'

Do I need to be a traditional architectural practice to support an apprentice?
No, employers can be any company that delivers on construction projects who are looking to support architecture apprentices. However:

- It is recommended that at least one member of your team be a registered architect in the UK.
- This individual is assigned as your apprentice's mentor.
- You must ensure that the apprentice can meet all the required KSBs in the standard.

4. Ethical considerations

Given the extent of current critical debates in the profession that can impact ethical practice, such as social responsibility, sustainability, inclusivity, professional conduct and the treatment of staff, you should assess any prospective employer's position on these issues before accepting a contract. Some employers will be heavily committed to delivering in certain areas, whilst others may be less clear. Some offices will also have internal working groups that you can join and this may be worth asking about in advance. For example, is there an internal inclusivity and diversity policy? Does the practice have a position on equal opportunities? Have they prepared an internal sustainability policy? Are they an RIBA Chartered Practice and do they adhere to professional ethics?

If your employer is an RIBA Chartered Practice, you are supported in the workplace under the RIBA Code of Professional Conduct, where your employer must have regard for your training and education.[4] For further information, you can refer to the RIBA's page on equity, inclusivity and diversity.[5] There are also lots of different external groups who promote equity and inclusivity in the built environment.[6]

During the application process, you may find yourself getting frustrated. Remember, if you do not find a job straightaway, this might not reflect your skills and abilities. Instead, it may be due to circumstances outside your control, such as an economic downturn or political circumstances. The RIBA provides updates on available apprenticeship jobs, which you can search for via RIBA Jobs.[7]

When supporting Level 7 apprentices in the office, the following describes some of the key criteria practices look for in an apprentice:

Practice perspective
By Marion MacCormick, Partner at Pollard Thomas Edwards, PTE

Commitment and **ability** are essential for a successful apprenticeship. Beyond that, it's about creating a match between the apprentice and the practice. At PTE, we look for individuals who have a passion for design, along with strong social and community values. It's a big commitment on both sides – our 'interview process' so far has been to employ the apprentice first, that way you really get to know each other and can see if it will be a good fit.

Figure 2.3 London South Bank University, Nelton Barbosa, architect at PTE, Woolwich Urban Village. Exploded axonometric from his final-year design thesis project.

Figure 2.4 Pollard Thomas Edwards, Brimscombe Port competition. Nelton Barbosa, architect at PTE, was an apprentice when working on the successful bid for the redevelopment of Brimscombe Port.

Making an application

Typically, apprentices make their application after one of three situations:

1. Enrolling directly after receiving an offer of employment.
2. Working for a practice for several years, then applying.
3. Seeking an employer after completing their year out as an Architectural Assistant Part 1.

This is not an exhaustive list, but these are currently the most common.

Once you have decided where you would like to apply, the next step is to complete your CV and portfolio. The RIBA has published guidance on Part 1 CV writing and, as with any job application process, there is no quick-win approach; however, there are ways you can try to maximise the quality of your application.[8]

Top tips for preparing your CV

- Create a template that provides information on your education, employment experience and interests.
- Write a short personal statement that introduces you and your skills at the top of your CV.
- Add employment experience and the responsibilities you have undertaken.
- Outline your key transferable skills.
- Feature a few examples of your best creative work.
- Proofread for spelling and grammar before submission.
- Include a cover letter with your CV.

Although cover letters may seem like an unnecessary formality, they are an intrinsic part of any application, since they provide an opportunity to demonstrate your suitability for the role, your experiences, abilities and professional skills. It is advisable that you tailor your cover letter to the role you are applying for, as 'copy and pasted' cover letters are obvious to employers.

Miles Brown

Address:

Mobile Number:

Email:

Personal Statement

An enthusiastic, determined young professional capable of balancing a passion for architecture, business, volunteering and the outdoors alongside a hard working mindset.

Education

BArch Architecture, Upper Second-Class Honours *with a Diploma in Professional Studies* Loughborough University	2022
A Levels, Design Technology A*, Geography A, Business Studies A Kings Priory School, Tynemouth	2017
Nine GCSE including English Language and Maths Kings Priory School, Tynemouth	2015

Professional Experience

Ryder Architecture   September 2022 - Present
Returning to Ryder as a trainee architect, working within the design team on multiple projects across a broad range of industries.

Ryder Architecture   January 2021 - August 2021
Part 1 Design Assistant, working on healthcare, commercial and residential projects ranging from RIBA Stages 2-5 such as Newcastle Pilgrim Quarter, Bank House and Friarage Theatres Hospital, notably being part of the bid-winning design team for Pilgrim Quarter development within the first month of placement.

RNLI Face-2-Face   Summer 2019
Playing vital role on Northern beaches, providing over 1600 safety messages and fundraising for the charity.

Loughborough University   January 2019 - June 2021
Architecture Open Day Guide.

ADP Architecture, Newcastle   July 2018
Week-long work experience understanding practice and REVIT for the first time prior to university.

Voluntary Work

Cullercoats RNLI Lifeboat Crew   July 2015 - Present
Inshore lifeboat crew fully trained in Maritime Search and Rescue skills with experience collaborating with multiple emergency services agencies in over 80 incidents. As well as offshore and advanced first-aid casualty care skills, the role develops my ability to work both independently and as a team player in real life experiences and scenarios. Awarded the Queen's Platinum Jubilee Medal as a frontline member of the emergency services having completed over 5 years of service.

Community project work in Peru   August 2016
Raising £4000 through numerous fundraising events, successfully constructing 7 greenhouses for a local community in the Sacred Valley during a 3 week expedition.

Community project work in Uganda   July 2009
Working alongside Watoto charity constructing a school room during a 3 week expedition.

Architectural Achievements

Member of winning team for Ryder Architecture Blueprint 2021 Design Competition

Nominated for Most Sustainable Design and Best 3D visualisation, 2020 Library

Nominated for Outstanding Year 1 Performance award, 2019

Participated in 2019 LUARC Summer School with Hiroshima Institute of Technology.

Other Qualifications

CITB - Health, Safety and Environment Test: For Operatives
UKSAR Medical Group - Level III Intermediate Casualty Care
Elementary First Aid Certificate
Gold, Silver, Bronze Duke of Edinburgh Awards
Full UK driving licence

Personal Achievements

Converted VW Caddy into campervan
Loughborough University Shooting Club Member
Scuba Diving with Poseidon Sub Aqua Club
Cycling - Mountain biking and downhill trails with race and marshall experience
Hill walking, winter mountaineering and climbing
Solo travel through Asia and Australia (March / April 2018)

Referees

Professional
Accademic

Figure 2.5 Miles Brown, typical CV for an architecture apprenticeship application. Note the need to balance written and visual content.

A few points when drafting a cover letter:

- Use words and phrases from the job description.
- Cover the essential requirements of the role.
- Try to include desirable requirements of the role.
- Keep it to a maximum of one-page.
- Proofread before attaching to your CV.

Further to the cover letter, some jobs require submission of your portfolio with your application. There are a few ways to approach this that will depend on whether you are applying in person or online. With the increase in digital platforms, there are plentiful ways to present your work beyond the traditional printed portfolio but remember that your work needs to be legible and of high quality.

Points to consider when preparing a portfolio:

- Do not include your full academic portfolio.
- Keep it between 20 to 30 pages in a format that travels easily.
- Include a range of skill sets from sketches to process work, as well as technical drawings and 3D work.
- Feature photographs of your architectural models.
- Showcase examples of your other creative work. For example, this could be photography, mixed-media, sculpture or film and video.

Once complete, review the original job description to ensure you have demonstrated the specific skills the employer is looking for and rehearse your presentation.

It is useful to note that you will likely have to tweak and revise your portfolio depending on the role and employer you are applying for. As outlined above, your cover letter should ideally respond to the specific job description of each role.

Preparing for an interview
When preparing for an interview, you should aim to research the practice in advance. A professional interview will likely be between 30 minutes and one hour.

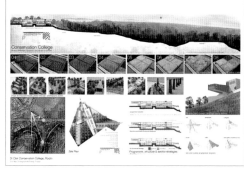
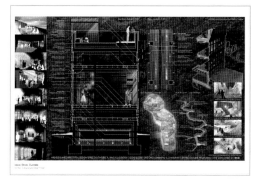

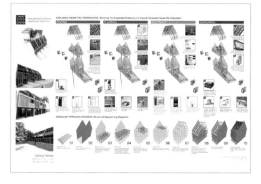
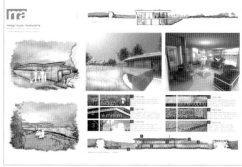

The employer might outline the practice's aims and ambitions, then move to a formal question-and-answer scenario. At this point, the employer will be keen to hear about your passion for architecture, your skills, abilities and fit within the office. As many businesses have adapted to hybrid working, it may be the case that your interview will be conducted online. If this is the case, try to have an online version of your portfolio that can be easily communicated. Make sure to download, install and have a basic understanding of the software that they would like to use in advance of your interview.

Figure 2.6 Timothy Welch, select graduate portfolio pages.
Note the composition of each page and the size of drawings and their placement.

Practice perspective: possible interview questions
by Patrick Devlin and Marion MacCormick, Partners, PTE

Here are a few questions that you may be asked at an interview. These are a great point of reference to help you prepare, but remember that you could be asked any range of questions, so be ready with your responses:

- What has been your experience in architectural practice so far?
- What skills have you developed?
- What skills do you need/want to develop?
- What has been your most rewarding experience in architectural education/practice so far?
- What do you hope/expect from an architectural career?
- What do you want to achieve in the short and long term in your architectural career?
- What do you know about our practice and what interests you about the work we produce?
- How will working here help you achieve the goals you have described?

Questions to ask at your interview
It is important to have questions ready for your interview, as it demonstrates your preparedness and eagerness to find out about the employer. You may devise questions during your interview; otherwise, it is advisable to prepare a couple in advance. Here are a few suggestions:

- What does the office team structure look like?
- What advice would you give to a potential new employee in your office?
- What is the practice's goals related to sustainability?
- Does the practice have a diversity and inclusion policy?

If you can attribute your questions to current debates in architecture, it can further demonstrate your awareness of current topics in the profession.

Receiving an offer of employment

If everything goes well at your interview and you are considered a good fit for the practice, you may be offered a Contract of Employment. Before you sign your contract, it is important to read and understand the terms and conditions of the offer.

Terms and conditions at a glance:

- Job title
- Salary
    - RIBA Chartered Practices are required to pay apprentices, at a minimum, the level set by the Living Wage Foundation[9]
    - Otherwise, you should be paid at least the National Minimum or National Living Wage for your age
- Contract start date
- Sick pay and procedures
- Other paid leave, such as maternity/paternity leave
- Working hours and policy on overtime
    - Check flexibility around key university deadlines
- Pension arrangements, mandatory or optional
- Probation period
    - Usually periods of three, six or twelve months
    - Check whether your role changes upon passing probation
- Termination procedure and timeline.

Further to the above, when agreeing employment terms, make sure you receive a written contract that identifies you as a permanent employee, so that you can complete your apprenticeship. Review the regularity of your wages and any other usual employment costs and check that the job role enables you to gain the KSBs required to complete the apprenticeship. Ensure that you are confident that your employer is happy to support you in combining workplace learning with formal academic training.

Every employer will have their bespoke contract terms and conditions, so it is important to understand what you are agreeing to and your rights. The *Architects' Journal* has published an employment guide, detailing what to look for and your rights.[10] You can also join the Section of Architectural Workers who are advocating for better working conditions in the profession.[11]

Remember, employers are required to offer you the National Minimum Wage as remuneration for your work. Later, we will outline the significance of the Training Plan, but note that your Contract of Employment, Apprenticeship Agreement and Training Plan are all different and must be treated as such. For more information on salaries in architectural practice, you can refer to the RIBA Salary Guide.[12]

It is also worth thinking about whether the job title aligns with your apprenticeship. We suggest that the title should distinguish between traditional Part 1 and Part 2 Architectural Assistant roles. As the title of 'Architect' is protected in the UK you cannot use it until you are registered with the ARB. For example, you **cannot** be called any of the following:

- Apprentice Architect
- Apprenticeship Architect
- Level 7 Architect.

However, you **can** use any of the following:

- Architecture Apprentice Level 7
- Architectural Apprentice L7
- Architectural Assistant.[13]

Remember, completion of the KSBs reflects your competencies and professional development, so should be recognised accordingly. Therefore, you should negotiate periodic points during your apprenticeship to review your progress and for it to be formally recognised through a salary increase commensurate with your increased competence and value.

Employers 'need-to-know'

Employing an apprentice:

- RIBA Chartered Practices are obliged to pay apprentices at least the National Living Wage (however, some agree to pay more). The RIBA recommends that all practices pay at least the minimum level set by the Living Wage Foundation.[14]
- Ensure the apprentice is paid for the time they are studying at university and that their salary is not reduced pro-rata (e.g. 0.8 full-time equivalent (FTE)).
- Provide an induction and on-the-job training.
- Extend the same benefits to apprentices as other employees, including sick pay, paid holiday and childcare benefits.
- Offer a pension scheme opt-in, if eligible.

Also consider:

- Incremental salary increases as the apprentice progresses through the course and their competence and responsibilities increase.
- A job title commensurate to their experience, beyond the traditional Part 1 Architectural Assistant title.

Once you have read the terms and conditions and are happy with the contract, you can sign and return it to your employer. After joining, spend a bit of time getting to grips with the office structure, working arrangements and getting to know your team. Once settled, it is time to find the right training provider.

Collating a Curriculum Vitae (CV) and portfolio

The next step is to find the right training provider. It should be noted that this decision formally rests with your employer; however, this important decision should involve your voice and interests. Many employers will appreciate this initiative and you need to find the best fit for *you*. The architecture apprenticeship is not offered at every architecture school, so you will need to conduct some outline research to see which schools are offering this route. Appendix B lists all schools of architecture currently offering apprenticeships. Some will have elements of their courses that appeal to you, whilst others may not. This is fine, as you need to enrol somewhere where you will be happy and get the most out of your learning opportunities, so this decision should not be taken lightly. When reviewing schools offering apprenticeships, consider your personal ambitions, whether the work aligns to your architectural and design position, and your career pathway for at least the next five years.

Figure 2.7 Northumbria University. End-of-year architecture exhibitions are an excellent way to get a feel for the types of work produced at a university and an opportunity to speak with graduates about their experiences.

When considering the right training provider, many apprentices:[15]

- spoke with colleagues in practice, recent graduates and those engaged in teaching
- visited different schools to meet the teaching team and see the school and wider university facilities
- received information from admissions tutors on course structure, content and teaching formats.

When deciding on what is right for you, think about the *ethos* of each school: What is their approach to architectural pedagogy and do their values align with your own? What is their approach to teaching – online, blended, on campus? How does the provider engage with critical debates in the profession and ensure readiness for practice? You need to be assured that you will be happy and supported at your chosen training provider. Remember that training providers can design their curriculum differently, so long as they adhere to the standard and meet the six hours per week minimum off-the-job training requirement. For example, below are three schools of architecture offering the architecture apprenticeship, each with their own approach to its delivery and management.

Table 2.1 Modes of apprenticeship delivery at different schools of architecture.

School	Schedule	Cohort	Taught
University of Cambridge	Two-week residential courses, three times per year	Distinct apprentice cohort	On campus
Northumbria University	One day a week	Partial integration with full time	Blended
University of Nottingham	One day a week	Distinct apprentice cohort	Blended

Beyond this, each will have its own modules, timetable, facilities and learning outcomes. All of which can influence your learning journey.

The right training provider at a glance:

- **Location**
  - Travel time to the university from home/from the office
  - Opening hours and access
  - Teaching structure: block, or weekly sessions
  - Days you are required to be 'off-the-job'
- **Size of architecture school**
  - Number of students/apprentices on the course
  - Number of staff on the course
- **Facilities**
  - What are the design studios like?
  - Is there a desk for every student, and storage?
  - What is the studio culture of the school?
  - What are the workshop facilities like?
  - What are the library facilities like?
- **Extracurricular activities (e.g. architecture society, sports, etc.)**
- **Studio structure and space allocation**
- **Integration with full-time and part-time students**
- **Types of project briefs**
- **Other modules that underpin design studio**
  - History and theory, technology, professional practice, media skills, sustainability
  - Is there the opportunity to choose optional modules?
- **Further institutional support available**
  - Health and wellbeing
  - Student support
  - Personal tutoring.

Schools offering the architecture apprenticeship have developed their own method of delivering the minimum of six hours a week off-the-job training (working at least 30 hours per week), which means that you will be learning in a different way to students on a full- or part-time course.

Apprentice top tips for deciding on the right training provider

- Meet with course leaders and discuss the course and modules.
- Consult training provider websites for current information.
- Discuss with senior colleagues and explore options together.
- Speak to enrolled apprentices to hear about their experiences.

The role of the End Point Assessment Organisation (EPAO)

If you already have knowledge of a training provider's role related to the EPA, you can move to the next section. We go into more detail about the process and requirements of the EPA in Chapter 3.

The final stage of your architecture apprenticeship requires the completion of the EPA. Some training providers are registered as End Point Assessment Organisations (EPAOs),[16] whereas others will have agreements with an EPAO external to their institution. An EPAO is a registered provider of the EPA. This registration entitles the provider to deliver the final stages of your assessment in an impartial and professional manner. The aim is to assess whether you have developed the KSBs detailed in the standard. All schools must have an in-place agreement with a registered EPAO. It is likely that your training provider will deliver this internally; however, there may be instances where you need to travel to another provider to complete your EPA.

It is the role of the EPAO to raise awareness of the process and to prepare the assessment. The UK Government urges all EPAOs to advise apprentices on the structure and assessment process of the EPA at the start of a programme. The aim is to ensure that you have adequate time to prepare for what is ahead and to demystify the process. All EPAOs must adhere to the following roles and responsibilities:[17]

- Ensure the gateway has been completed.
- Be aware of relevant professional body timelines and regulations.
- Promote services to employers, with details of the apprenticeship standards they are approved to deliver.
- Share service levels, setting out details on how they will work with employers.
- Take responsibility for confirming how costs will be calculated.

Although the EPA may feel a long way off, as an apprentice you should at least understand what the EPA is and how your chosen training provider conducts the process. This may not be a determining factor to influence your choice of university, but the delivery and timeframe between gateway and EPA could impact your learning at a critical stage. Therefore, you should obtain as much information as possible at the outset.

Career planning

As an apprentice, you will have little to no dealing with most professional bodies described in Chapter 1, but it is still worth acknowledging their professional requirements related to progression and career planning, particularly as you journey through the course.

Whilst the EPA measures occupational competences, it is important that your learning does not end with the completion of your apprenticeship. Your tripartite reviews will form an active part of your future planning, but it is urged that you establish an employer-led Continuing Professional Development (CPD) Plan that continues into the next five years of your career. Your employer may have an internal template that you can use to map your personal trajectory, so it is worth completing this and reviewing it every six months to one year. By focusing on your goals early on, you will benefit from a structured and reflective approach to your personal and professional development. Architecture necessitates an active approach to gaining new knowledge and skills to remain competent, so this will put you in good stead.

Figure 2.8 Bell Phillips Architects, team meeting. These are a key part of office life; it is recommended that you participate in them, as they are a great chance to present your ideas and offer feedback.

The initial skills assessment and Training Plan

Eligibility

Before spending time on your apprenticeship application, run a quick check to ensure you meet all the criteria to be eligible. The requirements determined by the UK Government are:[18]

- You must be 16 or over.
- You are not already in full-time education.[19]
- You live in England.

Requirements of employment at a glance:

- Get paid and receive holiday entitlement.
- Receive hands-on experience in a real job.
- Study for a minimum of six hours per week if you are working for at least 30 hours per week.
- Complete assessments during and at the end of your apprenticeship.
- Be on a career path with future potential.

Currently, apprenticeships in England are only available to those living in England and working on projects based in England for at least 50% of the time. Northern Ireland, Scotland and Wales offer their own apprenticeships, but none of them currently offer architecture apprenticeships.[20, 21, 22]

Entry requirements

Entry requirements for Level 7 architecture degree apprenticeships are set by individual employers in conjunction with the relevant training providers, but these must include a requirement for the minimum of an ARB-prescribed Part 1 qualification (or equivalent). At the point of application, your training provider will request the following information from you and your employer:

- An apprenticeship agreement between you and your employer.
- Your employment contract.
- Agreement with training provider and employer.
- A copy of your CV.
- Training Plan, agreed between you, your employer and the training provider.

The Apprenticeship Agreement at a glance:

This document must be signed by you and your employer at the outset of your apprenticeship and held by your training provider, and must include:

- your details (name, place of work)
- the standard and level: Architect (Integrated Degree), Level 7
- start and end date of your apprenticeship, including the EPA
- start and end date of the practical period of your training, not including the EPA
- duration of your practical training period
- amount of time to be spent in off-the-job training.

Figure 2.9 Hawkins\
Brown, London office.
A typical architectural
office environment that
you may find yourself
working in. Desks and
breakout spaces offer
diverse settings to
change the pace of
the day.

Initial Skills Assessment (ISA)

Once you have applied to your chosen training provider,
you will be asked to complete an ISA.[23] The ISA is required
as part of the apprenticeship funding rules and must be
accurately recorded by your training provider. The
requirements for the ISA are divided into two areas:

1. Level 2 English and maths.
2. Additional learning support or needs.

If you do not already hold Level 2 English and maths,
you will need to complete an examination. Some training
providers hold support sessions to help prepare you for
the exam, so it is worth checking in advance.

Further to the above, your training provider may accept
prior learning in other areas of the course. Prior learning
is deemed as education or learning that meets the KSBs
of the architecture apprenticeship. Prior learning does

not need to be educational experience but can also be training, qualifications, work experience and any previous apprenticeships. If you can demonstrate prior learning, it is urged that you speak to the training provider and pass any relevant evidence on to them so it can be reviewed against the KSBs (and Module Learning Outcomes) and recorded. If it is determined that your prior learning meets some of the criteria, you may be eligible for a reduction in weeks to complete your learning and a reduction in price (for example, if you have already completed a dissertation module, you would not need to take a further dissertation module). The findings from your ISA provide a baseline to help your employer and training provider create your individual learning plan for your apprenticeship. Moreover, your funding will need to be adjusted accordingly, so that it does not cover KSBs that you have gained previously.

Academic interview: virtual and face-to-face
Depending on the university that you apply to, you may be invited to attend an academic interview face-to-face or online. It is important to come prepared with the following:

- Your undergraduate academic portfolio, including drawings and models from two or three of your best projects.
- Any academic work that you would like to discuss, including essays, reports, case studies, group projects or competitions.
- Professional experience gained.
  - Note this is not necessarily a requirement, but experience as a Part 1 Architectural Assistant is strongly encouraged, before starting your apprenticeship.
- Any personal creative work, including paintings, sculptures, competitions, photography, etc.

The interview might last between 20 and 30 minutes with introductions, presentation of your work, interviewer questions and your own questions. If you are feeling nervous, remember the purpose of this interview is to celebrate your best creative work and professional experience. It is often a positive experience, rather than something to feel anxious about.

Before the interview, it is a good idea to prepare for possible questions that you may be asked, but also to prepare your own to ask. Here are some suggestions on those you may be asked:

- Why do you want to study an apprenticeship?
- What is your favourite drawing/model?
  Tell me a bit about how you produced it.
- What is the best thing about the practice you currently work at and what knowledge have you gained?
- What type of projects would you like to work on?
- What do you like to do outside studying?
- Which was the last exhibition you went to?
  Tell me a little bit about it.

Here are some questions you could ask at your academic interview:

- How many students are there on the course and how many are apprentices?
- Are apprentices integrated with full-time and part-time students, or run as separate cohorts?
- How is design structured: horizontal, vertical, super-studio?
- What internal support mechanisms are there for apprentices, such as wellbeing support?
- Does the university organise field trips, workshops or talks?
- What external engagement opportunities are there?
- Is there an architecture society? If so, what activities does it organise and is it funded?

Every individual's journey will be different, so before you apply it is always valuable to hear from others who have gained experience from the apprenticeship, whether this be other apprentices, colleagues in the workplace, mentors and even academics.

Apprentice top tips before enrolling and speaking to others

Anastasija Kostileva completed her apprenticeship in the 2022/23 academic year and has outlined three top tips for anyone considering enrolling on an apprenticeship:

1. **Get to know your apprenticeship peers** early on and set up ways to communicate outside the university. Being able to bounce ideas from one another is critical.
2. **Apply the day-to-day skills** that you develop in employment into academia. Time-management skills help you to organise and plan tasks in a similar manner to that of professional practice. Treat all your presentations as client presentations with strong research and design emphasis.
3. **Always ask questions.** If you ever feel stuck or unsure, always ask for help and never keep silent. Your tutors are there to support you with your academic work and can direct you to the right individuals; and your colleagues in practice are there to support you to learn on the job.

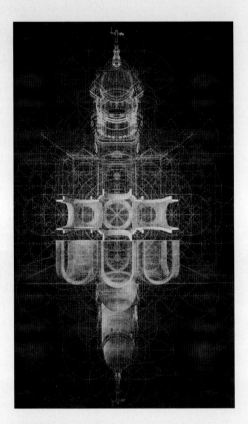

Figure 2.10 London South Bank University, Anastasija Kostileva, House of Government – A Second Chance. Final-year design thesis project.

Training Plan: defining roles and responsibilities

The Training Plan is an agreement that all apprentices, employers and universities adhere to at the start of every apprentice's journey.[24] The Training Plan is particular to the role of each member of the tripartite agreement (i.e. the responsibilities of the apprentice are different to those of the employer and training provider). It is important to establish and determine how all parties will work together to support you to complete your apprenticeship and achieve the standard. Every university has its own template, so it is urged that you read your responsibilities and understand how to uphold them. It is also good to know who to speak to if you have any issues in attaining/maintaining your commitments. Below are the points you may find in your Training Plan:

- Manage your learning to meet targets and deadlines, including submission of coursework and the EPA.
- Complete Level 2 English and maths.
- Engage with progress reviews to track progress and opportunities for enhanced learning.
- Manage and track attendance, informing your employer and training provider if you are going to be absent.
- Identify and raise any barriers to completing the course with your employer and training provider.
- Follow the student regulations (specific to your chosen training provider).
- Keep records of your off-the-job training.
- Participate in programme feedback and apprenticeship evaluations to support continuous improvement.
- Comply with policies and regulations set by your training provider related to your apprenticeship.
- Comply with policies and procedures of your employer on all matters concerning employment.

Support available to you

At one point or another, everyone will feel certain pressures of their course. Apprentices have reported experiences of stress, anxiety, burnout, depression and loneliness whilst undertaking their training. As the apprenticeship requires you to juggle academic, professional and personal life, it can be difficult to maintain a healthy work/life balance, so it is good to know where you can get support, should you need it. As an apprentice, you have access to the same support as any other student.

Every training provider will have their own internal support mechanisms. These services may be centralised within the institution coordinated by a wellbeing or student support team, or connected directly to the apprenticeship. Most academics are not trained in professional wellbeing support but will direct you to individuals who are. Moreover, many employers have internal support services to ensure their employees are suitably assisted. It is recommended to find out what additional support is available, beyond that of your mentor.

The following strategies suggested by Dr Jenny Russell can help you to find a balance between study, work and personal life:

Education perspective
By Dr Jenny Russell, Director of Education and Learning, RIBA

The route to qualification in architecture is demanding, not least for apprentices who are both studying and practising concurrently. While becoming an architect can be an immensely rewarding career path, it is also not without challenge.

The breadth of the subject is wide, and you are expected to be both creative and technical. This requires hard work and drive and, importantly, resilience. Developing strategies to balance your university study and practice-based responsibilities is vital.

- **Efficiency -** *work smarter, not harder*
  Understand what is required of you and make sure that everything you do subsequently serves that end. Consider how you can make use of the skills that you are gaining in practice within your academic work.
- **Productivity -** *develop effective time-management techniques*
  Set a realistic plan for getting through the work that builds in breaks, a social life, sleeping, eating and drinking, and other studying commitments. As an apprentice, time management is even more important as you balance your study and practice load.
- **Rationality -** *speak up and ask for help as soon as it is required*
  Don't be afraid to admit when things have become difficult and when you need help. Talk with your mentor and your tutor.
- **Effectiveness -** *focus on what you can control*
  Past a certain point, the effort you put in ceases to yield a worthwhile return. Learn to consciously recognise when you've reached that point.

Further information on these skills can be found in *Study Architecture Well* and *Practise Architecture Well*, published by the RIBA in 2021.[25]

What if things go wrong?
It is hoped that your journey as an apprentice is successful and that you find the right employer from the outset, but it must be noted that things do not always go to plan, so it is good to have sight of what to do should you need to change employer or training provider during your apprenticeship.

Change of employer
There might be any number of reasons that you will need to change employer. Some that have impacted apprentices to date include:

- economic downturn
- redundancy
- unable to demonstrate competency of necessary KSBs
- employer not the right fit
- communication breakdown.

If you experience any of the above, contact your training provider as soon as possible, so that they can intervene and help you move forward. If you are made redundant, there are two scenarios, depending on where you are in your apprenticeship:

1. **More than 75% of your training completed**
   If you have completed over 75% of your training or have less than six months left on the course, then you are eligible to continue your studies without having to find a new employer. The government will cover the outstanding costs of the remaining 25% up to 100%.

2. **Less than 75% of your training completed**
   If you have not completed 75% of your training, you can continue your studies for a further 12 weeks from the official date that you left your employer. Your training provider will likely have ways to support you in finding a new employer, but if you are unable to find an employer within the 12 weeks you must be recorded as withdrawn

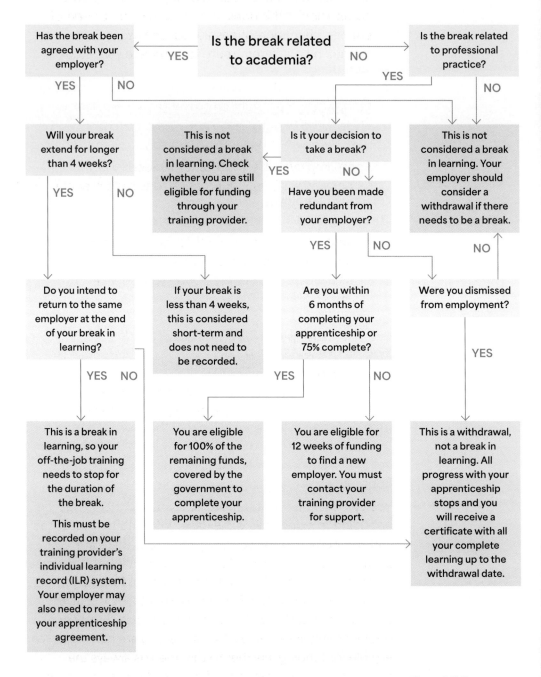

Figure 2.11 Flow diagram presenting routes available if required to change employer or training provider during your apprenticeship.

and provided with a 'record of apprenticeship partial completion'. If this does happen, you cannot re-enrol onto another apprenticeship, but can use your learning to enrol on a different route to complete your studies.

Employers 'need-to-know' for apprentice change of circumstances

As an employer, it is important to understand your responsibilities if your apprentice requires a break in learning. You must:

- notify the main provider that your apprentice will be absent for a duration or has left
- pause/stop payments through your service account
  - if the apprentice is taking a break from learning, pausing payments is required
  - if they are made redundant, payments must be stopped
- if there is a break from learning that lasts for more than 30 days, you must stop payments on the service account.

Change of training provider

You can change training provider if you find that things are not going to plan. If this is the case, you need to discuss this with your employer as soon as possible, as there are procedures to be followed as set in your Training Plan. If you find that the apprenticeship route is just not for you, you may be eligible to revert to a full-time or part-time course, but your apprenticeship will need to be terminated and your prior learning assessed. At this stage, you are no longer eligible for funding. Further to this, there is always the option to pause your studies, if needed. You can also take a break in learning with or without a break in work. Again, you must discuss this with your employer and determine the reason for your break in learning and the length of time you require. If it is for more than four weeks, then the off-the-job training must stop for the duration of the break. Once you

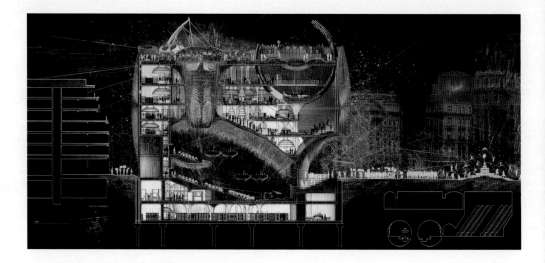

return to learning, your training provider will need to ensure that any training or assessment is replanned, but it is likely that it will need to align with the respective academic timetable of delivery. If you do find yourself in any of the situations above, it is strongly advised that you are honest and open with all parties involved in your apprenticeship and able to speak freely about your concerns.

The next chapter will detail ways to make the most of your apprenticeship, discussing employer-led learning alongside university-led learning, detailing modules, possible content and what to expect on your journey through the architecture apprenticeship.

Figure 2.12 London South Bank University, Timothy Welch, **Agora Anamnesis.** Longitudinal section through his final-year design thesis project at Piccadilly Circus.

3

Chapter 3
How can I make the most of my apprenticeship?

This chapter will detail elements of a typical apprenticeship course and indicate what you should expect throughout your learning. At each stage, we have provided tips and case studies to offer suggestions on how you can make the most of your journey. Remember that every apprenticeship is different, so to get the most from it you will need to be dedicated to the process.

This chapter will cover:

- support and guidance
- RIBA Themes and Values
- Part 3
- End Point Assessment (EPA)
- celebrating apprenticeship success.

Figure 3.1, based on Malcolm Knowles' five assumptions of adult learners (andragogy), outlines the required characteristics for apprenticeship success, each of which is likely to represent a step change from your undergraduate learning experience.[1]

1. Self-Concept
As an emerging professional, you will be independent and self-directed enough to make your own learning choices.

2. Adult Learner Experience
Your accrued experiences, whether educational, professional or personal, provide an increasing resource for learning.

Characteristics for apprenticeship success

3. Readiness to Learn
Your readiness to learn will be oriented towards what helps you thrive in your professional life.

4. Orientation to Learning
You will be more inclined to problem-based learning – new knowledge and skills that can be readily applied to your professional practical experience.

5. Motivation to Learn
You be motivated by internal factors, such as realising your creative, intellectual and social potential, opposed to external pressures.

Figure 3.1 Required characteristics for apprenticeship success. Derived from Knowles' five assumptions of adult learners.

Support and guidance

As an apprentice, you will not be short of support, but it is important to know the types of support available and how they can be accessed from the outset.

Types of support include:

- induction
- workplace management and mentoring
- objective professional opinions
- social enrichment and networking opportunities
- performance reviews
- mental health and wellbeing support.

Induction

Most employers will offer an induction for new employees. Even if you are an existing employee moving from a Part 1 Architectural Assistant ('year out') position to an Architecture Apprentice, you may need some initial support to understand your new role and responsibilities. Whilst induction will vary from employer to employer, you might find the following checklist to be a useful guide:

- Obtain a clear outline of your job role and responsibilities to help you understand what is expected of you. You will also want to determine expectations around dress code, time management and workplace behaviour.
- Find out how your role contributes to the wider team and where to go for support.
- Meet and, if possible, shadow key team members so you understand how your role fits within the wider practice.
- Arrange regular one-to-one meetings with your line manager.
- Obtain a welcome handbook or induction toolkit providing important information that will be useful for you in your first few weeks. It might include a glossary of key business terms, organisational charts and key tasks for you to complete in the initial weeks.
- Meet your workplace mentor.

You will similarly receive an induction from your training provider, with a mixture of both face-to-face and online activities. This may include:

- completing enrolment and collecting your Student Smartcard
- activating your IT account including email, virtual learning environment (VLE), student portal, apprenticeship management system (e.g. APTEM, OneFile or ePortfolio), Microsoft Office and mobile app
- timetable access
- meeting the academic team and your personal tutor
- meeting your fellow apprentices
- a tour of studio spaces, library induction and workshop induction.

Some of these activities are essential for you to complete and can only take place in person. If you opt to study at a distance, you will benefit from attending campus during induction week.

Top tip for induction

Many training providers have a student-run architecture society. By becoming a member, you will benefit from a programme of events from guest lectures, workshops and educational trips to mentoring opportunities and social gatherings, much of which can count towards your off-the-job training hours. Sign up at their Freshers' Fair stand during induction week so as not to miss out!

It is also important to know who fulfils specific roles in support of your apprenticeship, especially for those with Professional, Statutory and Regulatory Bodies (PSRB) responsibilities:

	Role / Description	Location		PSRB responsibilities	
		Employer	Training provider	PEDR	Progress reviews
Workplace management and mentoring	**Line Manager** Responsible for your workload, development and performance, and acts as a point of contact with senior leaders	●			
	Workplace Mentor Able to provide guidance, advice, feedback and support	●			●
	Employment (or PEDR) Mentor Oversees your professional practical experience and its recording	●		●	
	Apprenticeship Coordinator Oversees, coordinates and administrates the apprenticeship programme at an employer	●			
Objective professional opinions	**Professional Studies Advisor (PSA)** Provides an objective assessment on your professional practical experience		●	●	
	Apprentice Coach Assists your workplace mentor to maximise workplace learning opportunities		●		●
	Personal Tutor Able to provide pastoral and academic support		●		

Workplace management and mentoring

Line manager
It should be clear who your line manager is from day one. Your line manager should:[2]

- be aware of the requirements of your apprenticeship and ensure that the employer obligations to the Training Plan are fulfilled
- afford you sufficiently complex professional practical experience to develop the KSBs to achieve your apprenticeship and demonstrate the competency of an architect
- where necessary, coach you on how to carry out a particular task or allow you to observe the task being carried out and learn
- help you to understand your role and how it contributes to the projects that you are working on and the practice generally
- give you constructive feedback to help you identify where you are doing well and areas for improvement
- help you prepare for your EPA.

Your line manager is there to support you to develop and progress towards your apprenticeship. If you have any questions, concerns or issues with your employment or training, your line manager should be someone you can consult.

Workplace mentor
You may have a workplace mentor in addition to your line manager. A mentor is usually a colleague who you can talk to in confidence about your apprenticeship, and who should support you to raise concerns or make suggestions to improve your experience. A good workplace mentor can help you to settle into your new role quickly, thrive in the workplace, offer input to academic learning and make the most of your apprenticeship generally. Mentors need not necessarily be senior colleagues; those who have recently completed their own apprenticeship are especially well placed to take on this role.

Table 3.1 (opposite)
Roles and responsibilities of those involved in supporting apprentices.

Figure 3.2 Hawkins\ Brown. Workplace mentors should be generous in sharing their knowledge and experiences, and readily provide advice, guidance and feedback.

A workplace mentor may:

- share their knowledge and experiences
- provide advice, guidance and feedback
- offer encouragement and support
- promote and celebrate your success
- share development and networking opportunities with you
- help you to identify SMART goals as part of progress reviews
- support personal development and wellbeing.

Abby Aldridge, a former Architecture Apprentice, reflects on the benefits of having a strong relationship with her mentor, Andrew Drummond, Director.

Mentor relationship
by Abby Aldridge, former Architecture Apprentice, RH Partnership

Having a workplace mentor offers additional guidance and support, over and above that of academic tutors. This creates an opportunity for others in practice to participate in design reviews, show you additional precedents, or to simply offer words of encouragement to help with your studies. The sharing of knowledge is what makes apprenticeships so successful.

Employment (or PEDR) mentor

Your employment (or PEDR) mentor will directly supervise you and will have detailed professional knowledge of the work you undertake. They are responsible for reviewing and approving Professional Experience and Development Record (PEDR) sheets logged by you. Your employment mentor will:

- be an architect or cognate professional (such as an engineer, surveyor or project manager) involved in the design, procurement and management of the built environment
- possess at least five years' experience in the design of buildings and the administration of subsequent contracts.

Whilst it is possible for your line manager or workplace mentor to serve as your employment mentor, some apprentices have found it beneficial to separate these roles.

PEDR advice

Many apprentices find themselves time-poor and struggling to keep up with all the imposed PSRB reporting requirements, including the timely completion of PEDR log sheets. The following advice, while not compulsory, is intended to help you record the optimal amount of information in the most concise way possible:

- **Record your off-the-job training:** Include the amount of time spent in structured learning under 'Activities' (see Figure 3.3). This may substantially vary from sheet to sheet if you study via block release.
- **Detailed project descriptions:** It may be advantageous to outline the scope of works and form of appointment and, where appropriate, procurement route, type of building contract, consultant team and programme within 'Project Description' (see Figure 3.4, **1**). This will increase your commercial awareness and project management knowledge, and will be of use when preparing for Part 3 and EPA assessment methods.
- **List 'Project Tasks':** This can be done as bullet points, avoiding verbose prose (see Figure 3.4, **2**).

- **RIBA Plan of Work mapping:** record your professional practical experience against the relevant work stages (see Figure 3.4, ❸).
- **Reflective experience summary:** use the ARB Professional Criteria at Part 3 (PC1–5) (or equivalent KSBs (K12–K16, S12–S16 and B1–B7)) to structure your 'Reflective experience summary'. Again, bullet points will suffice.
- **Student / Employment Mentor Appraisal:** share headlines, including any identified skills and support needs, with your apprentice coach at the next progress review meeting.

Available online PEDR resources:[3]

- Student Guidance and FAQs
- Employment Mentor Guidance
- PSA Guidance.

Activities

General		
Annual Leave	64	Holiday
Bank Holiday	16	
Mentoring	4.5	Mentoring student intern during Part 1 studies
Mentoring	2	PlanBEE Meet the Employers event
Off the Job Training	1	Generative Design Tool - Unitize
Off the Job Training	1	Revit coordinates - LinkedIn Learning
Off the Job Training	2	Revit coordinates for Landscape Modelling
Degree Apprenticeship	99	Architecture Degree Apprenticeship at Northumbria University
CPD	1	West Kowloon Cultural District Authority, will present their ambitions for the district.
CPD	1	Active Travel in the Future City
CPD	1	Alternative Routes to Industry
Total:	**231**	

Figure 3.3 (above) Example PEDR log sheet. Excerpt of 'Activities' section, recording the time spent in structured learning.

Figure 3.4 (opposite) Example PEDR log sheet. Project entry, including detailed project description, list of project tasks and RIBA Plan of Work mapping.

Professional Experience and Development Quarterly Record Sheet

for the period between 21/12/2022 - 21/03/2023

RIBA 🏛
Architecture.com

Kate Baker   Stage 2 Experience

Project Details

Project Name:

James Cook University Hospital Life Cycle Works

Marton Rd, Middlesbrough TS4 3BW

 Project Description:

Client: James Cook University Hospital

Fee: £13,000.00

RIBA Stages: 3-6

Appointment: NHS Consultants Appointment

Design Team: P+HS Architects, Serco Limited

Project Brief: Refurbishment of existing staff changing facilities and medical records at James Cook University Hospital. Upgrades to finishes, fittings and services to improve outdated facilities.

② Project Tasks:

Drawings: Created a drawing package identifying works to take place including new finishes, furnishings and fixtures.

Meetings: Attended meeting on site to discuss project scope and requirements.

Technical: Produced sanitaryware schedule to replace existing

Site visit: I visited the site and completed a measured survey and used the 360 degree camera for recording.

Reviews: I participated in technical review with senior technician who amended and reviewed the drawings I had produced

Work Stages ③	2020 RIBA Plan Of Work	P	O
	3 Spatial Coordination	12	2
	Total	12	2

Apprenticeship coordinator

Apprenticeship coordinators oversee, coordinate and administrate the apprenticeship programme within an employer, reporting to senior management on progress and planning future development.

Objective professional opinions

Professional Studies Advisor (PSA)

Your training provider will appoint a member of staff to act as your PSA. They are typically staff with experience in teaching professional studies and monitoring students during their professional experience. Your PSA is similarly required to comment on quarterly record sheets.

How a PSA can work with you and your employer
by Wendy Colvin, Part 3 Programme Leader,
University of the West of England (UWE Bristol)

Gaining and logging practical experience is more than completing a PEDR log sheet and having this certified by an employer and PSA. The apprentice needs to have this experience reflected back to them, to see that this experience is good and to receive feedback about improving competency and meeting relevant KSBs. A PSA is well placed to provide this objective guidance. PSAs have a firm understanding of the threshold for registration and a wide exposure to apprentices based in many contexts. This, combined with the PSA as separate from the apprentice employer, allows for honest discussion with the apprentice about their progress towards qualification.

Apprentice coach

You will be assigned an apprentice coach[4] by your training provider. Your apprentice coach will work together with you and your workplace mentor to maximise learning in the workplace and support you in developing the necessary KSBs. Apprentice coaches are often seen as impartial and will typically have experience in coaching and/or mentoring.

Figure 3.5 Bowman Riley, progress review meeting. Most training providers offer the option to meet with your apprentice coach either in person or via video-conferencing.

You will meet every 12 weeks but, should an issue arise between meetings, you are encouraged to contact them. Progress review meetings are intended to:

- identify learning achieved from the start of the apprenticeship and between each progress review against the KSBs, through to the gateway
- provide your employer with guidance on how they can support you in the workplace to achieve required apprenticeship standards
- support you in developing SMART goals which stretch and challenge
- review attendance at scheduled structured learning and continued engagement with the programme outside of this, and the associated off-the-job training log
- review any available assessment results, including any late submissions and/or personal extenuating circumstances
- monitor your progress against apprenticeship milestones (annual progression, gateway, EPA and, where necessary, Level 2 English and maths)
- serve as first point of contact for safeguarding, prevent, health and safety, and wellbeing issues including key university policies related to these[5]
- support career development and aspirations.

Whilst your apprentice coach will review general academic engagement, progress and achievement, you are reminded that your academic tutors are best placed to advise and provide feedback on specific academic assessments.

Top tips for getting the most out of your progress review meetings
by Simon Kay-Jones, Professional Studies Coordinator for Degree Apprenticeships at London Metropolitan University

- **Focus on both the academic and practical:** Align your workplace reviews and PEDR log sheets to your progress reviews; this will enable you to use them as part of your workplace development and ensure that your employer is aware of your commitments and how to support you in advance of the review.
- **Budget time for you and your workplace mentor early:** Ensure you allocate ample time to prepare for and record your progression reviews. Book these in calendars for you and your employer at the start of the year.
- **Start noting your experience and progress early:** Develop a practice of keeping a folder of 'success stories'. This is mostly done by initiating a PEDR log sheet and recording them there, but can be done locally. Your apprentice coach is equally interested in hearing of your successes and challenges.
- **Define what 'progress' looks like:** Your apprentice coach, PSA and workplace colleague will be able to help you determine this with your contexts. Be careful not to place too unrealistic progression targets for fear of 'keeping up' with imaginary apprentices.

Personal tutor

You will be assigned a named personal tutor by your training provider as part of their pastoral and academic support arrangements. They will be a member of the teaching staff on the apprenticeship and will typically remain with you for its duration. You will likely first meet on a one-to-one basis in week one, as part of the induction process, and will subsequently do so periodically, including at your request. Personal tutors have access to your full academic profile and are therefore able to provide advice and guidance on a range of academic matters, including:

- progress
- performance
- study options
- good academic practice
- developing study, information and digital literacy skills
- signposting to centralised services (e.g. disability and dyslexia support).

Personal tutors will produce an agreed record of any relevant matters that arise during tutorials for the purpose of writing references, supporting cases of mitigating circumstances, audit, etc. If you wish for any matter to be treated as confidential, you should make this clear to them.

Social enrichment and networking opportunities

Recent cohorts of architecture apprentices have found the following social enrichment and networking opportunities have helped them settle into their workplaces:

- Meet current or past apprentices in your practice, with some smaller practices bringing together apprentices from across a region (e.g. RIBA East Small Practice Network).
- Attend networking opportunities with wider colleagues and relevant industry or professional bodies to support your development (e.g. the RIBA North East Young Architectural Practitioner's Forum (YAPF)).
- Attend regular team or practice-wide social activities.

The role of the forum in supporting emerging and newly qualified professionals
by Andra Antone, Chair of RIBA North East Young Architectural Practitioner's Forum (YAPF)

YAPF[6] helps improve and shape the opportunities available for young professionals and students in the construction industry in the North East. It is a multidisciplinary innovative group, strengthening conversations around current industry topics, forming a new and fresh regional culture. YAPF gives you the opportunity to stay inspired and engage with architecture beyond everyday work. This year, we look forward to exploring current topics and building relationships through art, culture, training and business events to inform how we learn, communicate and engage.

Figure 3.6 YAPF, panel discussion. KOPE, General Projects, Haptic Architects and Seratech discussing the prospect of a 'sustainable society' in the context of the climate emergency.

Performance reviews

Many employers find regular performance reviews a great way to facilitate communication with you and assist your personal development. They can be used to help you identify:

- the business objectives of your employer and your role in achieving those goals
- what skills and knowledge you need for the role
- areas you need to develop
- how well you are doing
- if there are any performance problems and how to address them.

There are typically three types of performance reviews:

1. **Regular one-to-one informal meetings** where your line manager will discuss your recent work and development. You should highlight any questions or concerns you may have about day-to-day tasks.
2. **Formal interim reviews** where your line manager discusses your progress against agreed objectives. Some of these reviews will also include your training provider.
3. **Annual appraisal review** where your overall performance is evaluated. This will include identifying strengths and areas for improvement, offering constructive feedback and helping with goal setting. These might also be used to review your renumeration and ensure that it is commensurate with any increased competence.

Mental health and wellbeing support

It is not uncommon to contend with some form of mental health issue, such as anxiety, depression or low mood, during your working life. Unhealthy perfectionism and difficulties in maintaining a reasonable work-study-life balance are common contributing factors within the sector.

Should you experience any of these during your apprenticeship, please be aware that the following services are available:

Table 3.2 Mental health and wellbeing services available to architecture apprentices.

Workplace	**In-practice Mental Health First Aiders** (where available)	• point of contact for employees experiencing mental health issues or emotional distress • trained colleagues offer an initial conversation through to assisting with access to appropriate professional support
Government	**Work Mental Health Support Service for Apprentices** (free service funded by the Department for Work and Pensions)	• emotional wellbeing support and advice • advice on simple workplace adjustments • successful coping strategies • a step-by-step support plan
Charities	**Architects Benevolent Society** (in partnership with Anxiety UK)	• dedicated Anxiety UK helpline • one-to-one therapy including counselling, Cognitive Behavioural Therapy (CBT) or clinical hypnotherapy
	Mind	• 'Infoline', offering confidential help for the price of a local phone call • 'Legal Line', providing information on mental-health-related law • Award-winning, PIF-Tick-certified information

RIBA Themes and Values

The RIBA's Themes and Values for Architectural Education, first outlined in The Way Ahead,[7] provide a renewed basis for the validation of schools of architecture in the UK and internationally.

They place increased importance on the social purpose of architecture, addressing climate change and responsible specification. They also ensure mandatory competence in designing for health and life safety, ethical practices and climate literacy, each of which has been designated as a mandatory competence for architects. This re-emphasis on the technical agenda of architecture needs to be balanced with innovative design skills expressed with visual acuity.

The six themes and values are:

E1. **Health and Life Safety**

E2. **Ethical and Professional Practice**

E3. **Structures, Construction and Resources**

E4. **Histories, Theories and Methodologies**

E5. **Design Processes and Communication**

E6. **Business Skills.**

Figure 3.7 (overleaf)
Overview of the RIBA Education and Professional Development Framework. Detailing Education Themes and Values, mandatory competences, CPD core curriculum and apprentice case studies, advanced study and specialisms, used as the structure for this chapter.

RIBA Education and Professional Development Framework

Education Themes and Values	Mandatory Competences	CPD Core Curriculum
E1. Health and Life Safety Expert contribution: Dieter Bentley-Gockmann, EPR Architect	**M1.** Health and Life Safety	**C1.** Architecture for Social Purpose
		C2. Health, Safety and Wellbeing
E2. Ethical and Professional Practice Expert contribution: Banah Rashid, Levitt Bernstein	**M2.** Ethical Practice	**C3.** Business, Clients and Services
		C4. Legal, Regulatory and Statutory Compliance
E3. Structures, Construction and Resources Expert contribution: Daniel Dyer, MawsonKerr Architects	**M3.** Climate Literacy	**C5.** Procurement and Contracts
		C6. Sustainable Architecture
E4. Histories, Theories and Methodologies Expert contribution: Stephen Smith, Wright & Wright Architects	**M4.** Research Literacy (potential future implementation)	**C7.** Inclusive Environments
		C8. Places, Planning and Communities
E5. Design Processes and Communication Expert contribution: Harbinder Birdi, Birdi & Partners		**C9.** Building Conservation and Heritage
		C10. Design, Construction and Technology
E6. Business Skills Expert contribution: Tim Bell, Melissa Dowler and Hari Phillips, Bell Phillips Architects		**B1.** Clients and Consultants
		B2. Teamwork and Collaboration

Apprentice Case Studies	Advanced Study	Specialisms
Laura McClorey FaulknerBrowns Architects + Northumbria University	*PhD (traditional or practice-based) or Professional Doctorate*	Academic / Researcher
Jack Davies Ridge and Partners LLP + University of the West of England (UWE Bristol)	RIBA Principal Designer Course	Principal Designer
Upinder Bahra Hawkins\Brown + London South Bank University		Client Advisers
Jacinta Barham Feilden Clegg Bradley Studios + University of the West of England (UWE Bristol)		
Daniel Kinghorn Leeds City Council + Northumbria University		
Sudhir Thumbarathy NORR / Ryder Architecture + Northumbria University		Sustainability Consultant
Katie Shannon Feilden Clegg Bradley Studios + Oxford Brookes University		Access Consultant
Delaram Nabidoost + Sarah Nottet-Madsen, HTA Design LLP + London South Bank University		Urban Designer
Cătălina Stroe Peregrine Bryant Architects + University of Bath	RIBA Conservation Course	Conservation Architect
Elizabeth Akamo Scott Brownrigg + Oxford Brookes University		BIM Manager
Oliver Howard Coleman Anderson Architects + London South Bank University	RIBA MBA	Sole Practitioner Practice Manager
Eleanor Lee GSSArchitecture + University of Cambridge		

How the RIBA Themes and Values might be reflected within the curriculum

Curriculum Example 1 (Northumbria University):
Yr 1
Authentic Design Inquiry (30 credits)
Architectural Research Methods (30 credits)
Yr 2
Design Project 3: Analysis and Proposal (40 credits)
Student Selected Investigation (30 credits)
Yr 3
Work-Based Practice Management and Law (30 credits)
Design Project 4: Realisation (50 credits)
Yr 4
Advanced Diploma in Professional Practice in Architecture[8]
End Point Assessment (30 credits)

Curriculum Example 2 (University of Nottingham):
Yr 1
Architectural Research Study (30 credits)
Building Case Study (10 credits)
Live Design Studio (30 credits)
Applied Architectural Technology (10 credits)
Yr 2
Culture and Context in Practice (10 credits)
Architectural Urbanism in Practice (30 credits)
Practice Research by Design (30 credits)
Professional Studies in Practice (10 credits)
Yr 3
Live Thesis Research (30 credits)
Live Thesis Portfolio (30 credits)
Reflective Practice Portfolio (20 credits)
Yr 4
PG Certificate in Professional Practice (60 credits)
End Point Assessment (30 credits)

We have used these Themes and Values to help you identify academic and workload learning opportunities to develop the necessary KSBs; invited industry experts to explain their importance and how they inform their own work; collated case studies to illustrate how other apprentices have done so; and identified Continuing Professional Development (CPD) opportunities.

Figure 3.8
Kolb's Experiential
Learning Theory.
Typical architecture
apprenticeship training
activities categorised
according to the theory.

As outlined at the beginning of the chapter, each apprenticeship journey will be different, as will some of the learning opportunities that will be extended to you. You will benefit from a combination of concrete experience, reflective observation, abstract conceptualisation and active experimentation (see Figure 3.8).

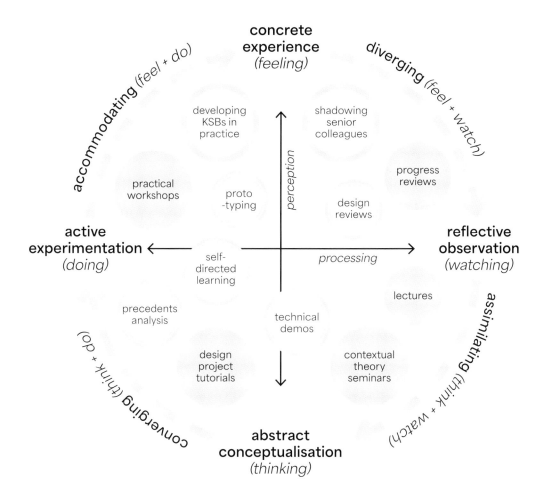

You will also be challenged to develop your non-dominant learning modes. Whilst perhaps initially uncomfortable, it will equip you to approach future learning situations with greater flexibility and confidence.

In addition to meeting the ARB Professional Criteria, the RIBA Themes and Values for Architectural Education expect Part 3 candidates to be able to demonstrate evidence of their understanding of relevant subject materials applied in practice, as follows:[9]

1. Architecture for social purpose.
2. Health, safety and wellbeing.
3. Business, clients and services.
4. Legal, regulatory and statutory compliance.
5. Procurement and contracts.
6. Sustainable architecture.
7. Inclusive environments.
8. Places, planning and communities.
9. Building conservation and heritage.
10. Design, construction and technology.

These ten topics also constitute the RIBA CPD core curriculum which will govern your Continuing Professional Development post-qualification.

The advanced study options and specialisms associated with each are discussed in the fourth and concluding chapter, *Professional Life Beyond the Apprenticeship.*

E1.

Health and Life Safety

Health and life safety requires architects to demonstrate 'authoritative knowledge of statutory frameworks to safeguard the community and end users',[10] and anybody potentially impacted by a project at any stage in its whole building life cycle. You should also consider how to study and practise architecture so that you look after your personal wellbeing.

At a glance:

- **KSBs:** K4, S5, K12, S13, S14, K15 & B1–B7
- **RIBA mandatory competence:** Health and Life Safety
- **RIBA CPD core curriculum:** Architecture for Social Purpose (C1), and Health, Safety and Wellbeing (C2)

Expert perspective
by Dieter Bentley-Gockmann

The *RIBA Health and Safety Guide*, authored by Dieter Bentley-Gockmann, EPR Architects, supports preparation for the forthcoming Mandatory Health and Safety test for architects.[11, 12] Dieter outlines why E1 is fundamental to the architect's behavioural, ethical and moral outlook:

Following the Grenfell Tower fire in 2017 and the subsequent introduction of measures to prevent such a tragedy happening again - including the introduction of new statutory designer duties under the Building Safety Act 2022 - understanding what it means for professionals to be competent, and seen to be competent in matters relating to health and life safety have been essential to restoring public trust in architects' and designers' ability to design safe, accessible and sustainable buildings. Ensuring buildings are designed to be safe to construct, occupy, manage and maintain is essential to ensuring a sustainable built environment that is robust and adaptable for the future.

Competence in health and life safety is essential for all our designers to ensure they understand and can meet our clients' aspirations to provide safe and sustainable buildings. An understanding and empathy for the need to balance safe outcomes with other competing project priorities, including time, cost and design innovation, is invaluable, as is an ability to demonstrate a proportionate and considered approach to safety in design. Competence in health and life safety equips designers with the ability to employ proportionate and innovative approaches to design risk management that balance the aspirations of clients with the needs of society and the aesthetic and technical aspirations of the design team to ensure that the built environment is accessible and safe, and feels safe, for all those that use it.

Architects have a commitment to promote positive social value through their work with the intent to improve society and an obligation to leave a place better than when they started. This, coupled with a duty to protect anyone who engages with their design, its construction and its use, is fundamental to any project and must not be taken for granted.

A demonstrable knowledge and understanding of health and life safety, including fire safety, are key parts of the practising architect's legal and ethical duty, meaning we must dedicate ourselves to making informed ethical choices and ensure that our decisions have positive influence on clients, project teams and suppliers. RIBA's Health and Life Safety test is for architects to demonstrate sufficient knowledge and professional care when working on design and construction projects, but is only the minimum requirement when protecting ourselves and others. In preparation for the test, it is recommended that you check whether your employer or training provider has a copy of the *RIBA Health and Safety Guide* and, if so, that you take some time to read it. The book has been structured using eight areas of RIBA's Health and Life Safety Knowledge Schedule including:

1. Preparation for site visits
2. Undertaking site visits
3. Site hazards
4. Design risk management
5. Statute
6. Guidance and codes of conduct
7. CDM Regulations
8. Principles of fire safety design.

In practice you will have access to the employer's archive of projects, delivered and speculative. Do not hesitate to review these projects and speak to your mentor about the specific strategies that were put in place to control and manage health and life safety.

Under CDM Regulations, your duties as a designer commence as soon as you start working on a design, which includes carrying out feasibility studies, competitions and concept design. It is necessary to try to eliminate risk as far as reasonably practicable, but where risk cannot be avoided, you must act to reduce and control it. Ultimately, reckless decisions can lead to injury or death and put the profession into disrepute. Although construction safety has significantly improved in Great Britain, 45 construction workers lost their lives whilst at work in 2022/23, whilst over 4,000 suffered non-fatal injuries.[13] If you are ever in doubt about issues concerning health and safety in the workplace and you feel you cannot speak to your mentor or a designated health and safety officer, you can contact the Health and Safety Executive. If you are concerned about health and safety on a project that you are working on, you must raise this with your mentor, even if it may be difficult to do so.

Top tip for visiting a site

If you are ever in a position where you have been asked to visit a site that you do not believe to be safe, do not go on site but instead report your concerns to your workplace mentor as soon as possible. Do not undertake any site visit alone and make sure that someone from your practice knows of your whereabouts.

Matthew Mayes, Architect, Director and Principal Designer at BDP, discusses why a good knowledge of building safety is necessary for all designers to help manage risks from the outset. A Principal Designer's role is to manage, monitor and coordinate health and safety during the pre-construction phase. This role is discussed in more detail in Chapter 4 (page 213).

A Principal Designer has an important role in influencing how the risks to health and safety should be managed and incorporated into the wider management of a project.[14] A beautiful building must also be a safe building. Safe design means the integration of control measures early in the design process, such as safe access to roof areas, safe access for cleaning, maintenance and replacement of façade elements, and safe access to plant equipment to ensure it can be safely maintained and replaced. Embedding this mindset into your thinking and designs from the earliest point is crucial to producing robust and safe design solutions.

Figure 3.9 BDP, apprentices discussing the relationship between buildings and their landscaping. Practice pin-ups such as these promote discussion and help boost your confidence when presenting to the team.

Practical knowledge and review of health and life safety issues in the office may occur daily, when designing buildings and spaces. Yet, how can this knowledge be transferred to your academic work? Typically, modules such as technology and professional practice are those where health and life safety competences are assessed. Assessments will be designed by your training provider and will be distinct for their course. They might take the form of a report, an essay or even an exam. For example, a report-based submission may require reflection on a previous (academic or practice) project design, reappraising its health and safety controls such as:

- pre-construction information
- identifying site issues and risks
- mark-ups on site plans and general arrangement drawings
- preparing a risk register
- risk management document
- construction phase plan.

Another possible assessment may be a scenario-based one to manage unforeseen issues on a site. For example, you might be required to responsibly manage hazardous materials on a site, detailing the steps that you would take and the individuals that you would need to engage. In contrast, for a technology module you may be asked to demonstrate the following in a supplementary report:

- construction logistics
- construction sequencing
- site management
- building maintenance
- protection from falling (Part K)
- fire safety and drawings (Part B)
- acoustics, ventilation and overheating (Part E, F and O)
- fire protection: materials, details and build-ups.

Beyond what you can expect from your employer and university work related to health and life safety, managing your own wellbeing on the course is also fundamental. In Chapter 2, we discussed what to do if things go wrong and, although you cannot plan for every eventuality, it is good to prepare as much as you can. The Architects' Mental Wellbeing Toolkit[15] is a great resource to monitor your personal wellbeing, but also to reflect on your rights as an employee and apprentice in university. Be a champion of good mental health and wellbeing practices and voice your concerns, to help us all to improve. It could even influence your design work, perhaps initiating wellbeing standards for a project or research into the impact of design on the wellbeing of its users.

The case studies that proceed this introduction to health and life safety present specific examples where apprentices have benefited from the reciprocity between workplace learning and university related to this theme. Each demonstrate the positive influence that the professional environment can have on supporting the development of conscientious and empathic emerging professionals.

C1.
Architecture for Social Purpose

Laura McClorey is an apprentice at FaulknerBrowns Architects and Northumbria University. Following her Part 1 Architectural Assistant training, Laura spent time working outside the profession, only to return to complete her studies as an apprentice. Laura outlines how this route enabled her to practise her passion, focusing her work on positive social purpose for communities.

The Degree Apprenticeship enabled me to develop my knowledge and skills to design and deliver spaces that bring social value in their contexts. I wanted to become an architect to deliver projects that convey positive social purpose and both my academic and professional work have championed this ethos.

My university thesis, Belfast Stories, centred on the design of a community and tourist-focused building in Belfast city centre. The brief focused on themes of urban regeneration and community engagement and – with tutor support – I was able to synthesise a project that was considered, through and through, 'of Belfast'. I was encouraged to undertake qualitative research with Belfast City Council members, citizens and local architects to develop a brief that was rich and true to the needs of the city. When it came to the technical delivery of the scheme, I sought to develop details that spoke of the city's history.

Without doubt, the apprenticeship enabled me to develop technically, becoming confident in discussing technical details with tutors, professional colleagues and my mentor. Knowledge and skills gained at university have translated into my work in practice, which has predominantly focused on public sector culture and leisure projects that deliver real social value to the communities in which they are based.

Figure 3.10 Northumbria University, Laura McClorey, Belfast Stories. Interior perspective of atrium, which is the adaptive re-use of an Art Deco bank to revitalise a city landmark but provide a civic gesture for Belfast.

Going forward, I hope to continue to work on public sector projects that can positively transform the lives of their users. Through the knowledge and experience I have gained over the past four years, I feel that I am better placed to both challenge and develop a brief to ensure that the ultimate design and programme is user-centric, inclusive and sustainable.

Rosie O'Halloran, Associate at FaulknerBrowns Architects, writes about Laura's extensive on-the-job experience so far:

Laura's interest in social value has supported the design and delivery of major community leisure and cultural projects. As a founding member of our Corporate Social Responsibility (CSR) group, Laura's impact extends beyond the buildings and places we create to improving how we operate as a practice.

Figure 3.11 Northumbria University, Laura McClorey, Belfast Stories. Exterior perspective illustrating how the project reinvigorates a key site in the centre of Belfast, connecting historic and cultural areas, and connecting people and place.

Associate Professor Kelly MacKinnon, Laura's tutor at Northumbria University, commends her academic work and indicates Laura's commitment to social value:

Laura's thesis project was the result of hard work of two years of study at Northumbria University. Following a RetroFirst approach, her proposal sensitively developed a heritage building in her home city of Belfast into a transformative civic proposal. The project looked to promote social value within the city by placing community engagement and reconciliation at the heart of its programme, something Laura has been an advocate for in practice. Laura's outstanding work and professionalism resulted in several regional and national awards such as Generation for Change (G4C) 2022 'Technical Apprentice of the Year' and RIBA North East Student Award Part 2 winner. She has since gone on to be a spokesperson for the apprenticeship route, being interviewed by 10 Downing Street and quoted by the Prime Minister's office.

Here are some suggested practice-based activities that might similarly help you understand the social value, and economic and social benefits architecture brings for individuals.

- Engage with role-modelling activities in practice.
- Review the United Nations Sustainable Development Goals and their impact on architecture.
- Participate in public exhibitions for practice projects.
- Join your employer's Equality, Diversity and Inclusivity group. If they do not have one, consider starting one.
- Sign the RIBA's Inclusion Charter.
- Support the RIBA mentoring scheme through practice.
- Engage with post-occupancy evaluations; monitor and review results with colleagues.

RIBA CPD core curriculum content (available on RIBA Academy):

- **Ethical Practice: Constructing sustainable communities** - enhance your knowledge of constructing sustainable communities, and consider finances, society and the environment.
- **An essential guide to community engagement and social value** - will engage and empower you to make value-based decisions to evaluate the social value of designs as people, as professionals and as part of their organisation.

Scan the QR code to visit the CPD page.

C2.
Health, Safety and Wellbeing

Jack Davies is an Architectural Assistant at Ridge and Partners LLP and is currently completing his course at the University of the West of England (UWE Bristol). Jack discusses how his work at Ridge has developed his site knowledge and awareness of health, safety and wellbeing, and its influence on his university design work:

I have been working as part of the architectural team and given design freedom with the support of the Project Architect for multiple office and workplace projects, logistic and manufacturing facilities. I am currently a part of the team designing high-quality retirement village projects at different stages, therefore I have a thorough understanding of the processes involved for site visits, organising internal and external meetings, speaking with the client, contractors and project managers to access information on project progress and RIBA Plan of Work programme, identifying requests for information (RFIs), project risks and site visit health, safety and information. These meetings help to understand the needs of the current work stage, whilst good records (meeting minutes) enable the team to understand the project's progress to identify possible hazards and determine the personal protective equipment (PPE), and safety measures to implement.

At Ridge we take part in continuous internal and external CPDs on health and safety along with company training for site visits, behaviours, and health and safety, which have been useful in understanding the different kinds of hazards and risks on site. I have developed my communication and notetaking skills, documenting progress through measurements and photographs with the contractor to highlight concerns that are resolved through sketches, conversations and annotations whilst on site.

When obstacles arise, I communicate with the site team and client to find solutions. Conducting multiple site visits has allowed me to understand the requirements of my role to be conscious of the safety of others and my own. Further to this, I have progressed my understanding of mitigating, and managing risks has also improved.

Regular meetings with the consultant team, clients and contractors have built my confidence to identify and raise risks with the Principal Designer, working as a team to find solutions. The apprenticeship has enhanced my awareness of health and life safety and these experiences have better placed me to critically examine my university projects, working through designs that attempt to mitigate risk, develop achievable construction strategies and managing production waste and hazards.

Figure 3.12 University of the West of England (UWE Bristol), Jack Davies, Mumbai Coastal Campus. Vertical circulation demonstrating key aspects of wellbeing design, particularly light and biophilia.

Alexander Miller, Partner at Ridge and Jack's mentor, outlines why apprentices develop a greater awareness of issues of health and life safety through engagement practice-based projects and engagement with consultant teams:

Through the apprenticeship Jack has built his knowledge and awareness of health, safety and wellbeing in a professional context. Ridge provides training for employees to understand construction risks and responsibilities, and the duty of care we have to building occupants and the public when delivering a project to the completion.

We encourage all team members to raise questions when they feel it is important to do so, and to ensure health and safety is our number one priority whilst the wellbeing of people is paramount in both our design activities and the way we deliver architectural services. Jack has taken this culture and learning through the apprenticeship course into practice, and considers the importance of health, safety and wellbeing as an essential aspect of the role of an architect.

Here are some suggested practice-based activities that might similarly help you understand your legal, professional and ethical duties in relation to construction site and workplace safety and wellbeing.

- Participate in devising a health and safety plan for a project.
- Review your practice's policies and procedures related to site conduct.
- Complete Construction Skills Certification Scheme (CSCS) training.
- Understand the responsibilities of different individuals as part of CDM Regulations.
- Keep up-to-date with Approved Documents on health and life safety, particularly related to fire safety.
- Engage in meetings related to risk management and help develop strategies to mitigate risk.

Scan the QR code to visit the CPD page.

RIBA CPD core curriculum content (available on RIBA Academy):

- **Health and Life Safety: Communication and coordination** - prepare for the RIBA Health and Safety Test, the CDM Regulations and the Building Safety Act 2022.
- **The RIBA Health and Safety Test** - will help to make sure you remain safe on site and can demonstrate that you are competent to design buildings that are safe to construct, inhabit, use and maintain.

E2.

Ethical and Professional Practice

Ethical and Professional Practice involves 'acquiring professional and communication skills to ensure projects are delivered with integrity and accountability within global, national and professional climate targets'.[16]

At a glance:

- **KSBs:** S4, K6, S6, K7, S7, K10, S10, K11, S11, K12, S12, K14 & B1–B7
- **RIBA mandatory competence:** Ethical Practice (M2)
- **RIBA CPD core curriculum:** Business, Clients and Services (C3), and Legal, Regulatory and Statutory Compliance (C4)

Expert perspective
by Banah Rashid

Banah Rashid, Project Architect and workplace mentor to an apprentice at Levitt Bernstein, explains why these skills and climate targets are important. The practice is a signatory of the RIBA 2030 Climate Challenge and of Architects Declare, and is a regular contributor to the Low Energy Transformation Initiative (LETI).

Understanding and designing for the issues surrounding the climate emergency is essential for all architects. This is a key driver for the entire profession, working to accommodate the current and future climate context by designing flexibly and with the view for adaptation over time. By changing our practices towards more sustainable approaches we can address and even embrace our accountability within the industry. Updating our design approaches can immensely and positively impact our future environment.

Learning about environmentally conscious design from the start of their architectural journey means apprentices can implement key considerations such as location, orientation, materiality, etc. into both their university and practice work. This knowledge will become embedded within their design skill set, ensuring that they approach all designs with sustainability as the foundation. Understanding and addressing these factors, alongside the wider social

Figure 3.13 LETI Guides: design guides produced by the Low Energy Transformation Initiative (LETI). They set out the approach, targets and benchmarks that developments in the UK need to achieve to reach net zero in operation.

Figure 3.14 Levitt Bernstein, Vorley Road, Islington. A mixed-use, net-zero-carbon and Passivhaus scheme for the London Borough of Islington.

and ethical issues, has the potential to enhance their input into projects in the short term and lead to future design innovations.

By learning the key factors for environmental design, they can begin to understand the long-term effects of their design proposals. Considering the whole-life carbon footprint of both their university and practice projects will ensure that sustainability is the main driver for their design decisions. Understanding and integrating these key skills during this early and conceptual-design stage of the apprentices' development will ideally lead to new innovations within the industry.

Examples of global, national and professional climate targets:

- **The Paris Agreement:** limit global warming to 1.5% above pre-industrial levels.
- **Climate Change Act:** reduction in greenhouse gas emissions by at least 100% of 1990 levels (net zero) by 2050.
- **RIBA 2030 Climate Challenge:** embodied carbon performance of <750 $kgCO_2e/m^2$ for non-domestic office buildings and <625 $kgCO_2e/m^2$ for domestic buildings by 2030 (minimum of 40% reduction compared to the current business-as-usual benchmarks).

Ethical and professional practice is similarly receiving greater focus in response to the Grenfell Tower tragedy, misconduct at some high-profile practices and architecture schools and, as highlighted by Banah, the urgency of the climate and biodiversity emergency.

You will see this reflected within your apprenticeship. For instance, and possibly in contrast to your undergraduate studies, you will find the need to demonstrate an understanding of the ethical issues and environmental sustainability more explicit in respect of design studio projects. It is not uncommon for sustainability to comprise an assessed criterion, with you being asked to declare a sustainability position, including any associated climate targets, as part of your design thesis project.

However, most opportunities to develop ethical and professional practice will be afforded within workplace settings.

As a minimum, and as has long been the case, you will be expected to uphold professional standards and behaviours in your interactions with society, clients and others.

The two most pertinent sets of standards are:

1.　RIBA Code of Professional Conduct[17] (or, Code of Practice for Chartered Practices)[18]
2.　The Architects Code: Standards of Professional Conduct and Practice.[19]

The former sets out the standard of conduct and practice that we are required to uphold and intends to facilitate critical reflection and continual improvement in respect of three principles:

1.　Integrity
2.　Competence
3.　Relationships.

Your employer will have a largely equivalent set of internal guidelines, outlining their values and commitments, as well as standards and expectations for employee behaviour. These are likely to contain guidance on developing open and transparent communications, promoting equality of opportunities and inclusive work environments, and encouraging diversity and inclusion. If you have not already done so, you would do well to familiarise yourself with these.

Whilst these are important, not least because breaching them can prevent you from practising, ethics in architecture extends beyond one's individual behaviour. There has been a relatively recent step change from personal to collective responsibility. For example, many practices, through initiatives such as Architects Declare,[20] are seriously considering their responsibilities towards global stewardship.

Similarly, and extending beyond efforts to minimise the environmental impact of buildings, the RIBA has made ethical practice a mandatory competence. To assist, they have developed a knowledge framework for the exploration of ethical thinking, reasoning and decision-making within architecture and architectural practice.[21] The inherent six duties for ethical practice, which are expanded upon in the *RIBA Ethical Practice Guide*,[22] are (examples of specific topics in parenthesis):

1. **Duty towards the wider world**
    (the environment; use of resources; and future-proofing)
2. **Duty towards society (and the end users)**
    (community engagement; social value; health and safety)
3. **Duty towards those commissioning services**
    (honesty; competence; and complaints)
4. **Duty towards those in the workplace**
    (equity, diversity and inclusion; good employment practice; and whistleblowing)
5. **Duty towards the profession**
    (reputation and value; promote high standards; and contribute knowledge through research and innovation)
6. **Duty to oneself**
    (principles and values; wellbeing and good mental health; and maintaining competence)

Top tip for your wellbeing

Do not forget to look after your own wellbeing and mental health by establishing a healthy work-study-life balance and securing good working conditions, including employment contract and appropriate, reliable pay.

Figure 3.15 Sheffield Hallam University, Tom Stovold, Care (In) Common: Establishing infrastructure of community care on City Road, Sheffield. A methodology for embedded care examining the changing role of architects in procurement and utilising collaborative design processes to maximise representation of community requirements.

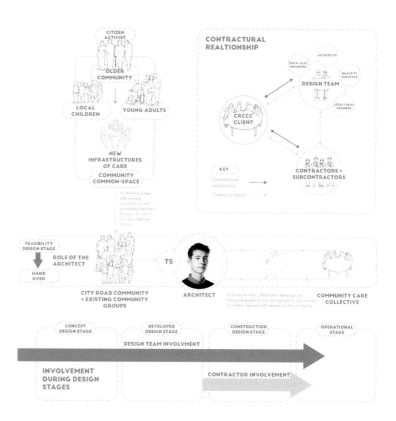

During your time in professional practice, you may have recognised that ethical practice distinguishes architects, particularly those who are RIBA chartered, from others involved in the design, procurement and construction of building projects. As an apprentice, proximate to industry, you are likely to regularly contend with ethical dilemmas in balancing climate and commercial imperatives. You may readily recognise some when your personal values come into conflict with what you are being asked to do, whilst others may be more subtle.

So, what ethical dilemmas may you face in practice? Here are three plausible scenarios:

1. Your practice is resistant to facilitate access to past projects for the purpose of post-occupancy evaluation as part of an academic assignment for fear of exposing problems.
2. In bidding for a project type in which your practice has relatively little experience, they ask that you include relevant projects on which you worked during your 'year out' experience with a competing practice.
3. A university client wishes to develop a new facility on the site of an existing building. Despite the existing building being high in embodied carbon and conducive to adaptive re-use, the client is insistent on a new-build solution.

How can you navigate such ethical dilemmas? The following steps, based on those recently shared with the profession, offer a considered approach:[23]

- **Reflect on the dilemma:** identify the facts and issues at play.
- **Identify what is causing the discomfort:** consider both your and your employer's values.
- **Understand your positionality:** how much agency do you have and how might inherent bias be affecting your view?
- **Check the relevant professional code:** is the situation you are facing covered?
- **Seek advice:** if the dilemma is still unresolved, proceed with care and discreetly enquire of others, such as your workplace mentor or apprentice coach.
- **Take further action:** if your concerns are supported, say something to a team member, client, regulator or institution.
- **Reflect again:** once resolved, ask yourself: What impact did my action have, and are there any measures that my employer could implement to prevent the dilemma from reoccurring?

Ethics is also a consideration in respect of any research you plan to conduct and will invariably require some form of approval. Most notably, you will typically be asked to consider the following principles:

- integrity
- justice
- non-maleficence
- beneficence
- respect.

Top tip for interacting with participants

You will need to be especially careful when interacting with participants. Research involving potentially vulnerable groups, such as children and young people, will receive greater scrutiny. Less so if you are making enquiries of fellow professionals.

Remember that many ethical situations will not necessarily have a 'right' or 'wrong' answer. Rather, you would do well to reflect on different interests, consequences and considerations, to reach an informed and balanced position. Over time, your training and experiences will allow you to critically reflect and position yourself as a practitioner within diverse forms of practice, and in turn influence how others view you.

Your competence in ethical and professional practice will ultimately be verified at Part 3 and the EPA, through scenario-based assessments, so you have plenty of time to develop this and identify concrete examples and, as an apprentice, you will have more opportunities than most. The following case studies share apprentice learning of the principles of ethical and professional practice amid changing operating models and legal, regulatory and policy frameworks that underpin business, architecture and construction. Both, assisted by their practices, are acquiring the needed professional and communication skills to ensure projects are delivered with integrity and accountability.

C3.
Business, Clients and Services

Upinder Bahra is a Level 7 Architecture Apprentice at Hawkins\Brown. The interdisciplinary practice offers specialist services in design for manufacturing and assembly (DfMA), urban data analytics and briefing and estates optimisation. Hawkins\Brown uses this experience to develop digital tools to drive productivity and value and deliver consistent project outcomes. Upinder is enrolled at London South Bank University (LSBU).

The AVA Footbridge is an adaptable, pre-manufactured footbridge system designed for Network Rail by a consortium of companies across architecture, construction and engineering and funded by Innovate UK. The design approach, utilising AVA's advanced configurator tool and essentially based on a 'kit of parts', allows communities and stakeholders to utilise a 'plug and play' system that configures in several ways to suit varying site and client requirements.

Involvement in early-stage RIBA Plan of Work activities to replace an existing footbridge at Stowmarket Station and improve step-free access and general pedestrian flow afforded me insight into interpreting and developing briefs, including an understanding of the client's commercial drivers and project aspirations, and experience in explaining design proposals.

Additionally, in working with the wider consultant team, I acquired a working knowledge of collaborative tools and platforms, and their role in coordinating design information and ensuring quality control. I also increased my knowledge of modern methods of construction and assembly, and associated technical design specifications.

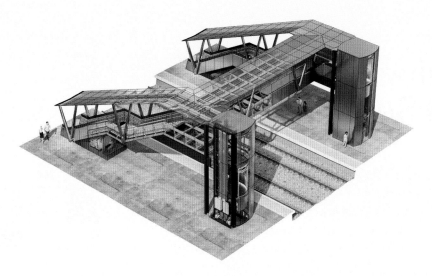

Figure 3.16 Hawkins\
Brown, AVA Bridge.
Axonometric of an
adaptable, low-carbon
and pre-manufactured
footbridge system,
described as a 'flat-
pack bridge' and
'market disrupter'.

This professional practical experience gave rise to an
emerging interest in modular and adaptable design.
Upinder explains how this was furthered through her
academic learning:

*My design thesis project – an architectural market hall
superstructure in Pesaro, Italy – similarly utilised a series
of adaptable and reconfigurable components to create
varying densities of space. I was also able to employ
what I had learned on the AVA project regarding circular
economy principles, robust and durable specifications
and reducing embodied carbon.*

Reflecting on her apprenticeship and future practice,
Upinder remarks:

*Having explored modular and adaptable design as part
of both my practice and academic learning, I would like
to develop my skills further. I considered emerging
technologies such as artificial intelligence (AI) within
my design thesis project. Through setting out a list of
parameters early in the concept design stages, I was
able to leverage AI systems to provide me with potential
architectural spaces created using a generic kit of parts.
I would like to learn more about how AI can optimise the
use of modular systems to provide us with the greatest
number of design options, especially where there are
budget and site limitations.*

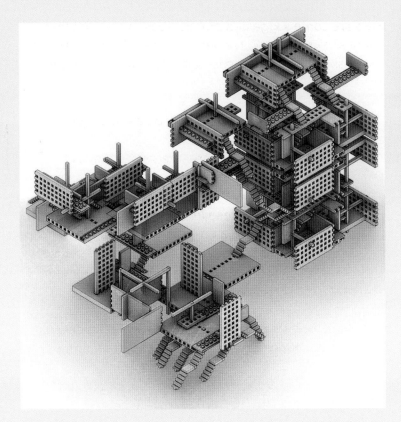

Figure 3.17 London South Bank University, Upinder Bahra, An Architectural Market Hall, Pesaro, Italy. MArch Studio 01, Super Structures set out to develop super-block, large-scale structures which would act as urban node, infrastructural or logistical interchanges.

Marco Vanucci, MArch Studio 01 Lead at LSBU and Director at Opensystems Architecture, believes Upinder's project represents a changing approach to how we might conceive of architecture:

Upinder's project explores the possibility to think and design architecture as made out of an economy of generic parts: she designed a 'kit of parts' that, while challenging architecture's part-to-whole relationship, flattens this hierarchy so that materiality, fabrication and assembly logics cater to a more flexible and less wasteful use of matter and energy. In this scenario, the project speculates that the use of artificial intelligence can help us gather vast amounts of data so that information about environmental and structural parameters, and material performance could be integrated into architecture.

Here are some suggested practice-based activities that might similarly help you understand the principles of good business practice and service provision, and the relevant legal frameworks.

- Complete workplace mandatory data protection (GDPR) training.
- Review contracts, client agreements and forms of appointment for projects you are contributing to and discuss any queries with your workplace mentor.
- Participate in project resource planning, monitoring and revision, including assessing resource against scope of services and contingency.
- Track the initiation and development of a project brief, recording the rationale for any changes.

Top tip: You may find your practice's project management system (e.g. Rapport3) useful to many of these activities.

Scan the QR code to visit the CPD page.

RIBA CPD core curriculum content (available on RIBA Academy):

- **Quality assurance systems: best practice guide to improving operational efficiency –** understand the role of quality management systems in improving practice effectiveness.
- **The RIBA Plan of Work (2020) –** expand your working knowledge of the Plan of Work, including how it can support whole-life thinking and greater strategic discussion.

C4.
Legal, Regulatory and Statutory Compliance

Jacinta Barham is a Level 7 Architecture Apprentice at Feilden Clegg Bradley Studios (FCBStudios). Since joining the practice in 2019, she has worked on a broad range of projects across the residential, mixed use, office and higher education sectors. Jacinta is studying the Part 3 curriculum at the University of the West of England (UWE Bristol).

The legal, regulatory and policy frameworks underpinning architecture can feel dry, disconnected or just complicated when taught abstractly in a lecture theatre. However, the apprenticeship has allowed me to put into practice my academic understanding and appreciation for their implications, with the professional practice models defining my daily project work.

Post-Grenfell, there has been substantial regulatory change to respond to shortcomings of the industry and transform fire safety in buildings. The Building Safety Act and Construction Product Safety legislation have prompted a growing demand for fire regulatory testing and certification of products in the UK.

Working on activities at RIBA Plan of Work Stage 5 for a large higher education project in Bristol, a key issue the project team faced was the lack of widespread testing of fire dampers across all partition build-ups. The possibility of specific condition testing was quickly dismissed as an option for resolution – due to both the extensive cost and considerably long timeframe which would be required that might lead to significant time implications on the project. Following many discussions with the project design team and relevant suppliers, the partition strategy design for the project was amended to align with the tested build-ups.

Figure 3.18 Feilden Clegg Bradley Studios, Temple Quarter Enterprise Campus, University of Bristol. The project team, of which Jacinta was part, were required to respond to industry-wide regulatory reforms.

Although simple in principle, this change involved a considerable amount of coordination between various parties and prompted the introduction of new wall types to the already substantial list.

My real-life exposure to this process highlighted the multifaceted nature of decision-making within the live project context, the importance of collaboration with various consultants to resolve complex design issues and affirms the importance of keeping up-to-date with legal, regulatory and policy frameworks.

Reflecting on the benefits of such learning, Jacinta believes:

Undertaking the apprenticeship has fundamentally better prepared me for a life in architecture. Experience of live projects or 'real world' scenarios like this one, when coupled with academic knowledge attained at university, work harmoniously together in developing essential skills needed to practise as a competent and well-informed architect.

Figure 3.19 Feilden Clegg Bradley Studios, Temple Quarter Enterprise Campus, University of Bristol: visualisation for a hackspace.

An intrinsic appreciation for the complexities of professional practice has instilled in me the importance of being up-to-date with relevant changes in standards or legislation; a skill I will hopefully be able to apply to my future practice and Part 3 qualification.

Carl Woodcraft, Associate, FCBStudios recognises Jacinta's development and its value to practice:

Jacinta's exposure to the practice of architecture, in parallel with her studies, has had an important impact on her architectural development. It has given her the ability to engage with complex technical issues in a much deeper way than is possible in an academic environment.

This is of real value to both Jacinta and our practice. Her learning can be immediately applied within the framework of architectural practice, which breeds confidence in her ability to contribute positively to conversations. In my opinion, this gives real value and validity to the design apprenticeship as a process, which I see as a wholly positive experience.

Here are some suggested practice-based activities that might similarly help you understand and keep up-to-date with the legal, regulatory and policy frameworks underpinning business, architecture and construction.

- Complete mandatory health-and-safety-at-work training.
- Attend a CPD session on the newly introduced Building Safety Act 2022 to understand how it relates to projects that you are working on.
- Prepare the health and safety file for a project you are working on and then review, update and revise it as the project progresses.
- Prepare a building regulations application, either for 'full plans' approval (large projects) or 'building notice' (smaller projects and works to existing buildings).

Scan the QR code to visit the CPD page.

RIBA CPD core curriculum content (available on RIBA Academy):

- **Principal Designer Handbook –** understand your appointment, competence requirements and statutory duties as a Principal Designer under the Construction (Design and Management) Regulations 2015.
- **Site inspection: ensuring delivery meets design – do you know the difference between supervision and inspection?** This module offers a brief history of the changes in law on inspection and looks at examples of identifying defects and practical site experience.

E3.

Structures, Construction and Resources

Structures, Construction and Resources requires architects to demonstrate 'climate literacy, responsible specification and ethical sourcing to enhance wellbeing, minimise embodied carbon, waste and pollution, and reduce demands on energy and water'.[24]

At a glance:

- **KSBs:** S5, K7, K8, S8, K9, S9, K10, K13, S13, K16, S16 & B1–B7
- **RIBA mandatory competence:** Climate Literacy (M3)
- **RIBA CPD core curriculum:** Procurement and Contracts (C5), and Sustainable Architecture (C6)

Expert perspective
by Daniel Dyer

Daniel Dyer, Associate and Certified Passive House Designer at MawsonKerr Architects, explains the importance of climate literacy to emerging professionals and how it is changing the design and procurement of buildings.

A significant portion of global emissions relates to buildings, from both the energy used to run them and the embodied carbon in their construction. Architects can therefore hugely influence both sources and are becoming adept at measuring, managing and reducing them. They are also growing in awareness of the wider material ecosystems, helping reduce waste, pollution and water consumption.

More and more, it is clients who are demanding sustainable buildings and are seeking architects who can design and deliver them on-site. To do this consistently, architects will need a core knowledge of engineering, materials and building physics.

Our clients want high-performance buildings which are delightful and meaningful to them. There is, of course, more to architecture than quantitative performance, so the challenge is to hit high performance targets whilst also creating architecture. This means having the skills needed to measure and manage quantitatively, without compromising on design. Ideally, designers will find opportunity in the constraints of performance, and a deep understanding of structure, engineering and material so that they can robustly collaborate with engineers and contractors to drive improvement.

Buildings have become complex systems with architects now supported by teams of specialist consultants and contractors to deliver them. To lead such a team, architects need knowledge of these specialisms, as well as first-principle knowledge of materials, sciences and engineering. As efforts to reduce carbon in construction begin to disrupt the complex assemblies of construction, it will be those with the strongest awareness of these core disciplines that most successfully transition to low-carbon construction.

Figure 3.20
MawsonKerr
Architects, Mount
Grace Priory Cafe.
This contemporary
building utilised unused
30-year-old boards
which were being
stored by the client at
a nearby location and
reclaimed stock of local
slate. This careful and
creatively considered
specification minimised
the use of new
hardwoods, low levels
of maintenance and,
when required, enables
repair and replacement.

The emphasis placed on climate literacy, responsible
specification and ethical sourcing represents the largest
step change within the RIBA Themes and Values for
Architectural Education and, indeed, the RIBA Education
and Professional Development Framework more broadly.
This is not surprising, given the role that the built
environment must play in responding to the climate and
biodiversity emergency.

In recognition of this, the RIBA has provided the following
guidance to help architects design within a climate-
conscious trajectory:

- RIBA 2030 Climate Challenge[25]
- RIBA Sustainable Outcomes.[26]

The RIBA 2030 Climate Challenge calls on members and
industry to adopt a stepped approach towards meeting net
zero whole-life carbon (or less) in the buildings they design
by 2030.

The RIBA Sustainable Outcomes are:

- net zero operational carbon
- net zero embodied carbon
- sustainable water cycle
- sustainable connectivity and transport
- sustainable land use and biodiversity
- good health and wellbeing
- sustainable communities and social value
- sustainable life cycle cost.

As part of the Graduate Attributes at Part 2, and in addition to applying the RIBA Themes and Values for Architectural Education, you will need to 'demonstrate ability to generate design proposals which integrate an understanding of *environmental building physics* and *comply with relevant statutory standards* to meet the RIBA Sustainable Outcomes Guide targets (including standards for zero carbon design)' [emphases added].[27]

Given the scale of this shift and varying levels of uptake, apprentices have reported disparity in the opportunities to develop these all-important competencies. On the one hand, those in design-led, environmentally conscious practices and working with progressive clients will likely have plenty of opportunities. Whereas those in more commercially orientated settings, with competing drivers, may have to think more laterally to obtain meaningful exposure.

Top tip for getting the right professional practical experience

If you find yourself in a workplace setting where opportunities to develop climate literacy is limited, you may seek a secondment to another studio team, as is sometimes possible within larger practices. Some apprentices have even secured secondments within sister or affiliated organisations to develop difficult-to-acquire KSBs.

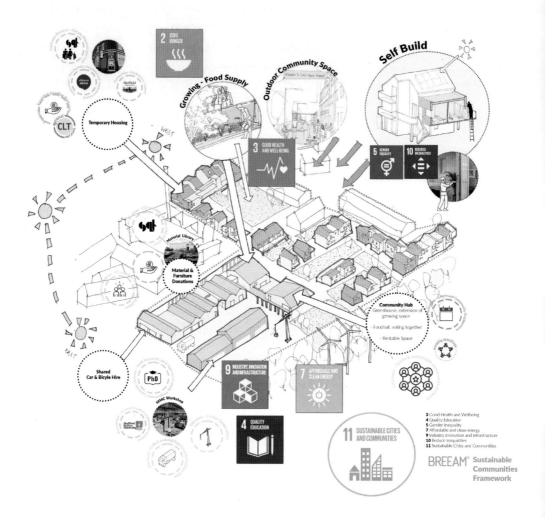

Figure 3.21 Sheffield Hallam University, Anna Dawson, The City of Sanctuary: A Community-Led Neighbourhood (Part 2 Presentation Award, RIBA Yorkshire Student Awards 2023). Apprentices are becoming increasingly familiar with the RIBA Sustainable Outcomes and are readily referencing the corresponding UN Sustainable Development Goals (SDGs) within their integrated design thesis projects.

In the absence of such opportunities, you will want to do your part in creating a culture committed to decarbonisation, regenerative design and advocacy. As suggested by *Architects Declare Practice Guide 2021,* initial steps might include:[28]

- Hosting a 'no-blame' democratic climate emergency roundtable discussion in your office to begin to align values.
- Reviewing and discussing the various frameworks and commitments available, mapping them against your practice's previous work, to find alignment or measure gaps.
- Carrying out a carbon footprint assessment of your office and its operations to measure business-related carbon impacts.
- Measuring project impacts by carrying out a full life-cycle assessment or whole-life carbon analysis for at least one project in each sector which your practice works in.

In the interim, the best route for some apprentices will be through integrated design projects, with some training providers delivering an ancillary taught module, whether formally assessed or not, in sustainable building,[29] energy and resource efficiency in design[30] or similar. Whilst all will introduce climate emergency fundamentals, you will need to undertake self-directed research and provide a considered response to (not exhaustive):

- human factors
- circular economy
- energy and carbon
- ecology and biodiversity
- water
- connectivity and transport.

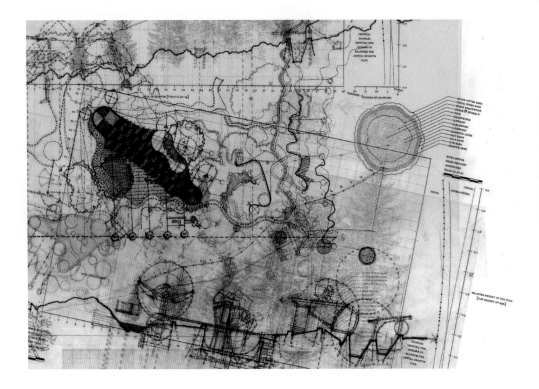

In upskilling, many practitioners and educators have found the following learning resources to be of assistance:

- Architects! Climate Action Network (ACAN)[31]
- Architects Declare Practice Guide 2021[32]
- Low Energy Transformation Initiative (LETI)[33]
- RIBA Academy[34]
- The Climate Framework[35]
- The Supply Chain Sustainability School.[36]

Additionally, *Designing for the Climate Emergency: A Guide for Architecture Students*[37] provides step-by-step guidance for creating sustainable designs:

1. Exploring your context – researching and analysing your site.
2. Defining a design concept, and creating values and goals.
3. Imagining climate emergency design strategies.
4. Testing and developing climate emergency design strategies.
5. Validating and communicating your approach.

Figure 3.22
De Montfort University, Liam Whittingham, *Healing the Nannau Estate.* Development of spatial and planted elements to immerse and educate visitors whilst protecting the landscape.

While you will recognise the inherent design process of the above, it is the renewed inflection towards sustainability considerations that may vary from your past academic and, even, recent professional practice experiences.

In support of your integrated design thesis project, you can expect your training provider to arrange for technical input, whether by means of tutoring or workshops, from specialist practitioners such as structural engineers, façade engineers, environment and sustainability specialists, modelled on advice in practice. Collectively, this depth of advice and insight is intended to enhance the technical resolution in this capstone project.

You should be particularly alert to the following training and upskilling opportunities – whether existing in academic or industry settings – to advance your knowledge and skills in sustainable practice:

- **Invited lecturers with expertise in sustainable architecture:** who will share stories of their sustainable projects and other exemplars.
- **CPD initiatives (see below example)**: share knowledge amongst your peer network, tailored to reflect your employer's current transition status.
- **Certified Passive House Designer Course:** which receives good uptake amongst apprentices nationally as part of their structured learning.
- **Ecology and biodiversity, and water management:** it can be especially difficult to access learning content for these.

Visits to Ruth Butler Architect and low-energy exemplar project
By Mollie Lord, Level 7 Architecture Apprentice, Lytle Associates and the University of Portsmouth

The purpose of these visits was to gain an introduction to Passivhaus design. Particularly beneficial to me was seeing the private residential project on-site, viewing the services installation, method of construction and discussing with the contractor and client the use of the Passive House Planning Package (PHPP). I have subsequently applied this knowledge to my workplace learning and enrolled on the Certified Passive House Designer course.

Figure 3.23a and b Lytle Associates, visit to Ruth Butler Architect and Low-Energy Exemplar Project. Visits to specialist practices and exemplar projects can help apprentices, and indeed all staff, raise their understanding of what is involved in sustainable practice.

We would encourage you to seize these opportunities afforded by your apprenticeship, advocate for sustainable or regenerative design solutions, and promote ethical sourcing throughout the life cycle of projects. And, have the confidence to challenge any long-standing norms you encounter.

The following two case studies share apprentice learning of the procurement processes and low-carbon and low-energy design. Both apprentices, assisted by their practices, are developing skills crucial to our transition to sustainable procurement.

C5.
Procurement and Contracts

Daniel Kinghorn is a Principal Design Officer at Leeds City Council, having completed his apprenticeship in 2023 with the support of Northumbria University. Daniel has taken part in several technical service procurement exercises, assessing private sector bids to provide technical support to the council on major strategic programmes.

During Leeds City Council's Throstle Recreation Ground project for 116 homes, a 65-apartment extra care scheme and associated landscaping, I took part in procurement activities. Being a local authority client, and with a contract value of circa. £40m, an Open Journal of the European Union (OJEU) compliant procurement process was required. The SCAPE Construction Framework was selected and a Direct Call Off undertaken. This meant that rather than a multi-stage tender with multiple potential parties (as with all previous tenders on the programme), a single contracting party was invited to undertake a feasibility study and submit a price with collaborative working between employer and contractor.

As part of the client team, I assisted in developing a brief, contributed to tender documents and took part in meetings and workshops with the tendering contractor and their selected consultant team. Through this, I was able to develop a range of knowledge and skills surrounding building procurement. Also, working client side, I was able to reflect on the position of a designer within the construction industry, and how being embedded within a client team assisted with the effective progress of the project and programme. Using the SCAPE framework limits projects to use of NEC contract forms, which further expanded my knowledge by building on JCT contract information gained through the Part 3 curriculum.

Working for a local authority client organisation has given me a broad range of experience in public sector procurement. I will be well placed to effectively assist clients work through the complex and highly regulated procurement landscape. Working in private practice, I would have a large range of knowledge and skills for preparing, submitting and supporting effective tenders or marketing activities to public sector bodies. I would be better able to define and work towards the goals of complex clients who have large stakeholder groups and assist a practice in defining and assigning appropriate resourcing to public sector tenders.

Reflecting on Dan's developing knowledge in construction procurement processes and building contracts, **John Stonard, Team Leader Design and Projects, Leeds City Council,** comments:

Dan has played an invaluable part in the delivery of this complex, high-profile project. Given previous restrictions on local authorities directly delivering housing projects, there is a dearth of relevant expertise. Dan's client-side role has provided key technical knowledge, enabling genuinely informed decisions to be made and an expert critical eye to be applied throughout the process. His specific knowledge has provided the bridge between local authority processes and the needs of a live construction project. This has enabled the right information to be provided, issues to be swiftly picked up, risks identified, etc. and has ultimately produced a better scheme.

Here are some suggested practice-based activities that might similarly help you understand the legal and regulatory basis of the procurement system.

- Familiarise yourself with the RIBA Plan of Work procurement task bar, specifically its influence on appointments, project programme and design responsibilities.
- Assist a senior colleague in undertaking a tender evaluation against the project award criteria.
- Consider the suitability of different procurement routes and their effect on the programme, cost, risk and quality of a project for presentation to the client.

Scan the QR code to visit the CPD page.

RIBA CPD core curriculum content (available on RIBA Academy):

- **Procurement essentials: procurement futures driven by collaboration** – understand modern approaches to procurement and contracting in a landscape characterised by rising costs, an increase in client demand and shifting policy requirements related to social value and net zero.
- **Project management: delivering high-quality outcomes** – understand key project management principles and processes from the initiation of your project, through to completion and use.

C6.
Sustainable Architecture

Sudhir Thumbarathy is a Senior Architect at Ryder Architecture, having completed his apprenticeship in September 2021 with the support of NORR (2018-21), Ryder (2021) and Northumbria University. The apprenticeship appealed to Sudhir as a route to registration in the UK – having worked as a technologist for two decades in the UK, Middle East and India – and an opportunity to enhance his knowledge of emerging trends.

The design of the apprenticeship allowed me to constructively align my design thesis project, student selected investigation[38] and professional practical experience to develop a well-rounded knowledge and specialist skills in climate science.

My research explored design and material decision-making based on heat loss analysis of existing building fabric, opposed to exclusively aesthetics and cost considerations. Furthermore, the embodied carbon associated with these materials was analysed to allow design teams to choose materials that have a reduced environmental impact such as natural rather than oil-based products. My research concluded that whole-life carbon understanding and analysis should run parallel to the RIBA Plan of Work stages, arguing that the earlier this is addressed the more significant the carbon reductions are.

Dr Zaid Alwan,[39] Associate Professor in Architecture and Built Environment at Northumbria University and Sudhir's supervisor, remarks:

It is this optioneering at the early stages of the design project that is key to minimising both operational and embodied carbon over the lifetime of a retrofitted building.

Whilst this is typically the domain of mechanical or building services engineers, such analysis within architecture practices has become key to meeting low and zero carbon targets and addressing carbon obligations.

Sudhir was able to utilise this knowledge in practice by streamlining and incorporating sustainability goals within practice processes, including its application to a sustainable exemplar project (net zero impact in use), the Stephenson Building at Newcastle University.[40]

His knowledge and skills were formalised through One Click LCA and Certified Passive House Designer training and resulted in him being appointed to NORR's International Sustainability Research Group.

Recognising the value of Sudhir's apprenticeship, his former workplace mentor **Robin Stewart, a NORR UK Director,** remarks:

The combination of academic knowledge and professional practice experience enhanced our service, providing our clients with comprehensive sustainable information to make informed decisions benefiting their projects and the environment.

Figure 3.24 NORR UK, Stephenson Building, Newcastle University. The project marries a refurbished modernised original frontage with a highly contemporary extension, utilising a timber structure and CLT timber floor plates and highly efficient building materials.

Reflecting on the benefits of the apprenticeship to his future practice, Sudhir says:

Since joining Ryder, I have been afforded opportunities to further enhance my climate science skills through formal training on specialist thermal bridging software, Flixo, as well as to develop strong leadership skills.

Overall, the apprenticeship has equipped me with up-to-date knowledge and skills in sustainable design, fire and life safety and other important competencies. This has enabled me to make informed and responsible decisions in respect of project briefs and client needs. I believe a knowledge of Passivhaus design principles and carbon emission calculations are crucial to delivering the required change in the profession and wider construction sector. I feel confident that my expertise will help minimise negative impacts on the environment and am keen to encourage others to adopt a climate-conscious trajectory towards reaching net zero.

Here are some suggested practice-based activities that might similarly help familiarise you with the principles of climate change mitigation and adaption, low-carbon and low-energy design, over the life cycle of a building, and help you acquire skills in effective client briefing and management.

- Prepare a client communication seeking their commitment to the ambitions of the RIBA 2030 Climate Challenge[41] and provision of first-year operational energy and potable water data to a project.
- Host a workshop with a client and project team to agree an approach to materials and circularity.
- Employ free-to-use embodied carbon calculators[42] to help develop alternative material specifications for a project you are working on.

Scan the QR code to visit the CPD page.

RIBA CPD core curriculum content (available on RIBA Academy):

- **Low-carbon design, technical features and the performance gap -** understand how low-energy, fabric-first design can reduce construction and operational costs.
- **High-performance, human-centred, healthy design -** sustainability is more than energy efficiency and carbon impact, it is also about considering the impacts on our environment and how the environment we create for ourselves impacts on us.

E4.

Histories, Theories and Methodologies

Histories, Theories and Methodologies advocates 'critically analysing and researching narratives and cultural, environmental and social values in architecture to understand and extend architectural pedagogy'.[43]

At a glance:

- **KSBs:** K2, S2, K4, S4, K11, S11 & B1-B7
- **RIBA mandatory competence:** Potentially the subject of a fourth, *Research Literacy (M4),* at a later date
- **RIBA CPD core curriculum:** Inclusive Environments (C7), and Places, Planning and Communities (C8)

Expert perspective
by Stephen Smith

Stephen Smith, Partner at Wright & Wright Architects, explains how a critical, research-informed approach is fundamental to the practice's projects in the culture and education sectors. Wright & Wright Architects are adept at identifying how architecture can give resonant expression to clients' broader institutional aims and ambitions.

History and theory provide a rich reference point for the way we design and how we understand the context that we are working in. History is at its most potent when we consider it as our shared history: how have certain patterns of use been established and evolved over time, and how might they change? Theory, through precedents and an understanding of the deeper meaning of design philosophies, gives both a grounding and a launching-off point for ideas.

Our clients are usually at a point of transition when they approach us with a brief. The catalyst might be a need for space or a desire to transform a set of buildings that have fallen into disrepair. It can be hard to find a starting point at times, but by looking carefully at the history of a site or how a building has evolved, a strong dialogue can emerge about what to retain and what can be changed, why certain materials have been used and how they might be used in counterpoint with the new.

Figure 3.25 Wright & Wright Architects, St John's College Library and Study Centre, Oxford.
A discreet, connective element situated between historic quadrangles and landscaped gardens.

*An understanding of history and theory can help give
perspective to an architect: whilst some aspects of society
can appear to be moving very quickly, there are other
fundamentals that remain more constant and slowly
evolving in the history of architecture that can help to
give balance.*

You will have received a fundamental education in the
history and theory of architecture at undergraduate level.
A good provision would have included the teaching of
histories of architecture – both Western and non-Western
– and its cultural, environmental and social contexts, and
critical engagement with contemporary issues. Ideally,
you will have had an opportunity to apply this knowledge
to your studio-based design projects, evidencing your
developing critical thinking and creative practice.

Within your apprenticeship, there will be further
opportunities to hone your research and critical thinking
skills by reflecting upon and interpreting theories of
architecture, most notably within your design thesis project
and dissertation (or equivalent), and ideally developing an
individual philosophical approach to architecture. As the
role of research-led design methodologies is discussed in
E5. Design Processes and Communication, we have chosen
to focus on research methodologies here.

Invariably, there is a need to evidence independent learning
through research and advanced scholarship as part of a
Master's-level qualification and an architecture
apprenticeship is no different. This has traditionally involved
a dissertation, but its format has evolved to reflect changing
epistemologies and learner diversity. It is likely to assume
one of two formats:[44]

1. **Traditional written dissertation (typically 8,000-10,000
   words):** akin to a humanities or social sciences discipline
   and utilising argument, evidence and data.
2. **Research project report (reduced word count):**
   alternative format, supported by experimental,
   speculative and artefactual outputs as part of one's
   creative practice.

It is worth noting that the research project report has proved popular amongst apprenticeship cohorts with multiple intelligences. For example, drawings, models, photography, installations and digital media have been well employed by those with dyslexia. This format does not exclude the need for writing altogether, as an accompanying commentary, together with full documentation of the practice-based research output, is required and provides an opportunity to develop writing skills. The equivalence to which the creative practice and artefactual outputs may substitute for words will be agreed with your supervisor.

To help you determine which format is best for you and align to your forte, and as a general introduction to architectural research methods including critical writing, literature reviews and methodologies for primary exploration, we recommend consulting the following key texts:

- *Architectural Research Methods*
  (Linda Groat and David Wang, 2013)
- *Research Methods for the Architectural Profession*
  (Ajla Aksamija, 2021)
- *Creative Practice Inquiry in Architecture*
  (Ashley Mason and Adam Sharr, 2023).

Whilst dissertations might have traditionally been associated with historic and theoretical discourse, today – at least, at their best – they look to balance this with architectural research aimed at addressing an issue of general concern within the architectural community, ensuring relevance and impact. Most training providers allow apprentices to choose the topic of their dissertation, but may typically include:

- architectural history and theories
- climate change
- cultural diversity
- design approaches
- design and construction techniques
- environmental and social sustainability
- issues in practice
- social justice.

Top tip for maximising enjoyment from the apprenticeship

You are more likely to do well, and indeed enjoy it, if the subject of your inquiry relates to an emerging interest, your own cultural perspective or something that has sparked your curiosity during your apprenticeship. This can help you define your own identity and positioning as a future architect.

There is a concerted effort amongst many training providers to better integrate design and research. However, even in the absence of this, it is not unusual for apprentices to constructively align their design thesis project and dissertation, allowing them to investigate a complex question from two lines of inquiry. Figure 3.26, borrowing from the work of Christopher Frayling[45] and Nigel Cross,[46] illustrates the interrelationship between design and research in the pursuit of architectural knowledge.

There is a perception that architecture apprenticeships are less theoretical. This is untrue, although admittedly apprentices have less time for theoretical inquiry. That said, many do choose to adopt a more pragmatic, practice-

Figure 3.26 Ashraf Salama (adapted), The Designerly Ways of Knowing. Design uses research to improve and expand the level of knowledge utilised, and research uses design to close the gap between theories and real-life situations.

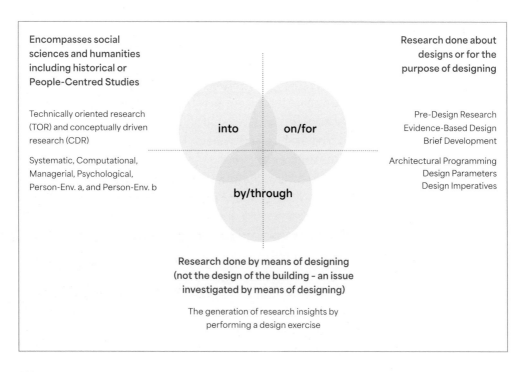

Encompasses social sciences and humanities including historical or People-Centred Studies

Technically oriented research (TOR) and conceptually driven research (CDR)

Systematic, Computational, Managerial, Psychological, Person-Env. a, and Person-Env. b

Research done about designs or for the purpose of designing

Pre-Design Research
Evidence-Based Design
Brief Development

Architectural Programming
Design Parameters
Design Imperatives

into

on/for

by/through

Research done by means of designing (not the design of the building - an issue investigated by means of designing)

The generation of research insights by performing a design exercise

focused approach to architectural inquiry, being more interested in the practical application of a theory.

This is well illustrated by these recent research-based inquires undertaken by architecture apprentices nationally, each of whom drew on the expertise and opportunities in their workplace:

- **'Immersive Technologies and the Evolution of Healthcare',** Emmanuel Akintayo, Leeds Beckett University / Gilling Dod Architects (see Figure 3.27a and b)
- **'101 George Street, Croydon: A study into the benefits and challenges of Modern Methods of Construction to deliver sustainable housing in the United Kingdom',** Anthony Miller, London South Bank University / HKA
- **'To what extent does school building design impact on the behaviours and behaviour management of pupils in English secondary schools?',** Amy Rumbold, Northumbria University / NORR Consultants Ltd.

Figure 3.27a and b
Leeds Beckett University, Emmanuel Akintayo, Immersive Technologies and the Evolution of Healthcare. Artist's impressions of Greater Manchester Mental Health Centre utilising contemporary immersive technologies and a traditional Nightingale Ward.

Amy Sullivan

We would encourage you to seek opportunities to share and disseminate your research, whether through conferences or publication. Some apprentices have recently had success in publishing written and drawn outputs, whether from extended essays or dissertations, within academic and disciplinary journals. One example is Amy Sullivan, whose extended essay, 'Could We Work Less?' was published in *BUM Edition 6: Order.*[47]

The knowledge and skills that you develop in research literacy, and indeed any findings, have the potential to extend beyond the academy. In recent years there has been an increasing engagement with research by practices in the pursuit of their social and environmental principles, often in collaboration with universities, clients, consultants and contractors, with some practices employing in-house research assistants and/or associates to oversee such activities. Examples include:

- 'Zero carbon buildings in changing climates', Knowledge Transfer Partnership (KTP), FCBStudios / University College London (UCL).[48]

Figure 3.28 *BUM Edition 6: Order*, Amy Sullivan, 'Could We Work Less?' An investigation of John Maynard Keynes' essay, 'Economic Possibilities for our Grandchildren', in which he predicted that we would need to work as few as 15 hours per week today (illustrations by Erica Borgato and edited by Lee Marable).

- 'Can new-build homes in the UK help older people to age-in-place?', Doctorate of Philosophy (PhD), ID Partnership / Northumbria University.
- 'Closing the Loop: Circularity in the Built Environment', collaborative research publication with various partners, Ryder.[49]

Figure 3.29 Oxford Brooks University / FCBStudios, Katie Shannon, Principles of Anti-Ableist Design. Diagram of architectural factors and their effect on disabled people.

The following apprentice case studies share acquired knowledge and skills in developing and implementing inclusive design strategies and methods, and in creating successful buildings, within the context of neighbourhoods, towns and cities, one of which has plans for dissemination amongst the wider architectural community.

C7.
Inclusive
Environments

Katie Shannon is a Level 7 Architecture Apprentice at FCBStudios with a passion for combatting ableism in architecture and its impact on the disabled community. She adopts an intersectional 'anti-ableist design' approach to prioritise the accessibility of buildings and the built environment more widely. Katie is currently undertaking her EPA with Oxford Brookes University.

The interplay and exchange between practice and academia that the apprenticeship model affords positively informed the development of my inclusive design skills, through both my academic research and workplace CPD.

The landscape of legislation in the construction industry surrounding accessibility is shifting. I was able to keep an awareness of, and engagement with, emerging guidance and legislation, such as PAS 6463 and the introduction of adult changing places. At the same time, I studied existing research into ways disabled people interact with the built environment and conducted interviews to forge new ways in which this relationship can be improved. Understanding intersectionality between physical disabilities, sensory disabilities, and cognitive and mental disabilities, presents both design problems, but more importantly, opportunities for innovative and creative design solutions. Experiencing academia and practice together was key to developing knowledge of diversity, flexibility, choice, community and joy, with regards to designing for disabled users.

Although the architectural profession is changing for the better, there are many ways in which we could be doing more for disabled people. My goal going into Part 2 was to establish clear principles for what I call 'Anti-Ableist Design', a theoretical design philosophy which addresses inequity in the build environment with regards to elements such as

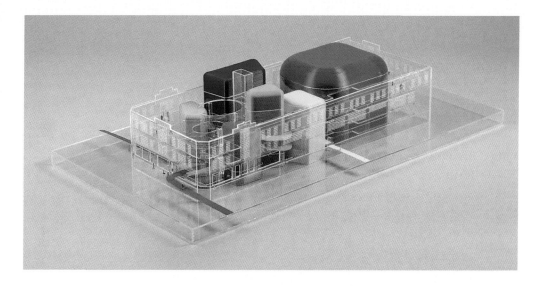

Figure 3.30 Oxford
Brookes University,
Katie Shannon,
Anti-Ableist Theatre.
Model for an Anti-
Ableist Theatre, set
within an existing brick
warehouse building.
The coloured and
textural wayfinding
system is represented
here in the colourful
inserts into the
transparent backdrop
of the existing building.

wayfinding, sanitary facilities, auditoriums, entrances, public space, fixtures, fittings, lighting and acoustics, through the prioritisation of facilities and spaces which create comfortable and joyful experiences for disabled people.

Commenting on how she might further develop these interests as part of her future practice, Katie says:

FCBStudios presents opportunities for workplace research, therefore I am pursuing a proposal to create an all-encompassing inclusive design framework that builds upon the foundations of the Anti-Ableist Design Guide[50] produced during the apprenticeship. This will enable projects to be assessed for their inclusivity and suggests ways in which inclusivity can be improved upon. The aim is to embed inclusive design more intrinsically into the practice's design process, and ensure mechanisms are in place to maintain and improve our competencies. It is my hope that through the implementation of the inclusive design framework, FCBStudios can effect positive change in the wider industry.

Reflecting on how Katie's practice-led research has benefited the practice, **Isabel Sandeman, Architect and one of two Apprentice Mentors at FCBStudios,** says:

We have benefited enormously. Practically, we now have access to Katie's Anti-Ableist Design Guide, alongside an inclusive CAD library of underrepresented groups for the practice's general use. In a more philosophical sense, Katie's knowledge and enthusiasm for the subject, which she has presented both internally and externally, has demonstrated the need for all of us to do better. We look forward to incorporating Katie's inclusive design framework into our project work, and hope that as with FCBS CARBON, it might become available for use by the wider architectural community.

Figure 3.31 FCBStudios, Immersive Digital Exhibition Space, Cornwall Museums. Creating an interactive and multifaceted approach to interacting with museum objects and content, including touch tours and quiet rooms, as well as step-free access, audio tours and changing places.

Here are some suggested practice-based activities that might similarly help you understand the legislation and principles that apply to creating inclusive environments which meet the diverse needs of people who want to use them.

- Familiarise yourself with the Inclusive Design Overlay to the RIBA Plan of Work.[51]
- Work with the Inclusive Design Lead on a project to undertake an inclusive design audit of the building, either mid-build or pre-completion, and provide a report against the Inclusive Design Strategy.
- Enquire about the option to volunteer as the Inclusion Champion for a smaller-sized project you are working on and help raise standards of equality, access and inclusion.

Scan the QR code to visit the CPD page.

RIBA CPD core curriculum content (available on RIBA Academy):

- **An inclusive approach to neighbourhoods of the future –** learn how to design and specify healthy and inclusive buildings that go beyond Part M and deliver much more than regulatory compliance.
- **Designing for Neurodiversity: making informed design decisions –** an accessible guide to neurodiversity and design, debunking technical terminology and illustrated with best practice case studies.

C8.
Places, Planning and Communities

Sarah Nottet-Madsen and Delaram Nabidoost are newly qualified architects at HTA Design LLP, having passed their EPA at London South Bank University in February 2023.
The practice has a strong record of designing and delivering better homes and residential neighbourhoods, and initiated the Housing Quality Indicators[52] and Design for Homes.[53] Having joined HTA in 2014, Sarah has prepared Design and Access Statements for a variety of regenerative masterplans. Commenting on her role in one project, Winstanley and York Road Masterplan, Clapham Junction, Wandsworth, Sarah says:

It was crucial that the statement captured the project's key objectives, including the retention of family homes, a sustainable mix of housing tenures and sizes, and the provision of significant cultural and community resources.

The collating of a Design and Access Statement is a useful exercise for developing your understanding of the planning policy framework. Given the breadth of content, it can also help familiarise you with the project beyond your own involvement.

Much of this learning has proved transferable to Sarah's academic work. For example, her initial academic design and award-winning project, 'Land and Sea: An Interface Pathway'[54] was similarly informed by an understanding of place and well narrated.

Dela has found her involvement in the projects at Chelsea Court and The Lakes Estate, together with the subject of her Case Study Report, particularly insightful:

Working on these regeneration and refurbishment projects has allowed me to better understand the needs and aspirations of communities, and space and building users. Moreover, as both schemes are designed for less privileged end users, my inner interest in helping communities is fulfilled by doing our best to provide a lovely place for the residents to call home.

For example, we were able to reconfigure the existing accommodation at Chelsea Court, designing high-quality units benefiting from improved sizing, outlook and consideration of current and future needs.

I have especially enjoyed engaging with and understanding different stakeholders and their needs through community consultation activities. This approach was intrinsic to the development of a range of affordable house types at The Lakes Estate, Milton Keynes in close collaboration with existing residents and Milton Keynes Council. This also extended to estate-wide improvements to existing parking, play spaces, cycle connections and landscaping.

I have learned a lot by working with a practice responsible for pioneering the practice of 'Community Architecture', considered avant-garde until only relatively recently. Additionally, our Monday design review sessions allow us to present work to the partners and broader team, having a dialogue to ensure every scheme is well-designed, organised and responsive to the stakeholder needs. These include suggestions of innovative design engagement techniques to enable a contribution from the communities we serve which enhances their experience and improves the product and outcomes.

Sarah and Dela continue to take full advantage of opportunities at HTA. Sarah, having recently been promoted to a Project Leader and tasked with coordinating RIBA Plan of Work Stage 3 activities for the Gascoigne East Phase 3B masterplan, is using her experiences to help architectural assistants develop their own skills in the writing of effective Design and Access Statements. Dela has been appointed as one of the architects working closely with the contractors

to deliver The Lakes Estate RIBA Plan of Work Stage 4 production information pack.

Reflecting on their professional development, **Caroline Dove, Partner,** comments:

Sarah and Dela have managed to balance their university studies and work at HTA Design LLP, due to their exceptional organisation and time-management skills. Sarah's experience at HTA, prior to starting her apprenticeship, has enabled her to hone her skill set, taking her knowledge and understanding of the built environment and applying this to her university projects. Whereas Dela's knowledge and understanding of the built environment developed rapidly during her apprenticeship, enabling her to elevate her professional work at HTA.

Figure 3.32 HTA Design LLP, The Lakes Estate. The scheme comprises 589 new sustainable homes and was the first designed to 2019 Plan:MK standards.

Here are some suggested practice-based activities that might similarly help you understand the legal, regulatory and policy frameworks for creating successful urban and rural places, and the relevant planning processes and procedures.

- Research best design practices for changing demographics, ways of living or public health issues for a project you are working on.
- If working on a large, complex project, develop the Design and Access Statement (DAS) in partnership with the Inclusive Design Consultant (or Access Consultant).
- Plan and deliver a community co-design workshop to better understand the community's needs and aspirations. You may find the book *Collective Action!: The Power of Collaboration and Co-Design in Architecture*[55] inspiring.

Scan the QR code to visit the CPD page.

RIBA CPD core curriculum content (available on RIBA Academy):

- **Place making, what's the future of place?** - better understand the cultural, social and environmental challenges of shaping places, and integrate public realm, movement planning and urban design in your practice.
- **Planning Essentials: A toolkit for preparing planning applications** - do you find the planning system overly complex task frustrating? This module offers strategies for leading engagement with the planning process.

E5.

Design Processes and Communication

Design Processes and Communication is 'critically evaluating authentic aesthetic, compositional and spatial principles to synthesise socially, ecologically and environmentally sustainable integrated studio projects'.[56] Design encompasses an extensive part of the role of the architect and is also a principal aspect of architectural education. How design is interpreted can be expressed in a variety of ways and pending on who you ask, may be defined differently. Both your employer and training provider will have specific ideas on what design is to them and their own methodologies, but as an emerging professional, it is important that you establish your own position.

At a glance:

- **KSBs:** K1, S1, K3, S3, K8, S16 & B1–B7
- **RIBA CPD core curriculum:** Building, Conservation and Heritage (C9), and Design, Construction and Technology (C10)

Expert perspective
by Harbinder Birdi

Harbinder Birdi, Creative Director at Birdi & Partners and Visiting Professor to the Department of Architecture at Cambridge University, discusses why design is a necessary part of an apprentice's suite of skills. Harbinder is an advocate of collaborative practice and outlines why design that benefits from wider inputs helps generate more collaborative teams and successful projects.

Design remains critical to the success of contemporary professional practice, particularly as more diverse routes open and more complex issues emerge; as the climate emergency forces our hand and the way that we source, use and re-use materials is called into question. Design is the holistic bond that integrates intellectual and critical activity, and the design studio remains the setting for this collaborative and inquisitive dialogue to flourish. With time, styles, techniques and challenges may change, but the pedagogical underpinning of design requires creative imagination, innovation and representation skills all in support of architecture for positive purpose. As the construction industry changes to suit the diversity of clients' needs – from planning through to post-occupancy – the architect must also adapt to remain relevant. The apprentice who has day-to-day exposure to the different aspects of design practice, and who can collaborate with a versatile team of people, will gain valuable knowledge and skills to produce informed design practices, addressing current legislation and needs.

Moreover, if they can work cohesively with interdisciplinary teams problem-solving issues related to climate literacy and resource efficiency, building safety and legislation, inclusive design, and the social and ethical purpose of projects, then their input will be invaluable. The empathetic apprentice, ready to listen and share ideas with others, is more likely to succeed in practice and better realise their potential as a changemaker to solve some of the critical questions we face.

Design and the design studio remain intrinsic to the practical training of an architect. It is the chance to explore your ideas and for them to flourish; to test and experiment. The apprenticeship is no different, as design constitutes 50% of the curriculum for all RIBA validated courses. This means that you will design at varying scales and complexities during the different stages of your journey. There is a distinct step change between the work completed during your education at Part 1 and Level 7. Whilst undergraduate education focuses on the principles of design and improving problem-solving skills, Level 7 is more oriented toward the exploration of ideas and research through design, 'understanding how the boundaries of knowledge are advanced through research, to creatively synthesise complex environmental, social and spatial issues, showing originality and the use of hypothesis in the application of knowledge' being undertaken 'at, or informed by, the forefront of the academic and professional disciplines'.[57]

Figure 3.33
De Montfort University, Mehul Ashok Jethwa, Resilient Horizons: Safeguarding Suffolk's Historic Coastal Villages from Climate Change (Postgraduate Winner, AJ Student Prize 2023). Evolution of building and site migration as the landscape floods from 2023 to 2063, illustrating how design influences sustainability and communities.

Whether you are on a day release, block or residential model, you will need to engage with the design studio. Many schools integrate modules that underpin the design studio, such as technology, professional practice, sustainability, and history and theories, and you will have the chance to explore their value through a design idea and its synthesis. You will be tasked with more than one design module during your apprenticeship, but the most significant of these will likely take place in year three of your apprenticeship and will establish your trajectory as an emerging professional. The opportunity to explore a research question, in-depth and without constraint, incentivises inquiry and can frame your outward position. Although you might not feel that you have as much time or freedom to challenge a brief as your full-time colleagues, there are plenty of other ways that you can explore design ideas, benefiting from the support of your employer:

- Reappraising a site from your practice's archive (recent or not). Enabling access to preliminary information such as site drawings, surveys, scans and topographical studies.
- Constructing a design brief associated with key debates within your practice. This may be linked to function, organisation or technological strategy.
- Tapping into the range of expertise in your practice. Those with specialist knowledge could offer distinct feedback on aspects of your work.
- Engaging with a community group or client that your employer has worked with previously, identifying a specific project brief.

How you integrate knowledge gleaned from practice into your designs will depend on the types of projects your practice delivers and the extent to which they can offer you their resources. It is strongly encouraged to discuss your ideas with your mentor before using any information from your employer's archive. Remember, certain projects may be subject to copyright or confidentiality. It is always better to seek approval than risk issues arising later.

Top tip for developing your brief

Whatever topic you choose to explore through your design projects, be sure to investigate those that are most significant to you. Beyond the tutorials with your tutors and mentor, you should remain abreast of contemporary issues in the media across diverse areas such as politics, climate, society, economics and culture. At Level 7, your designs must present a critical position on a specific topic with a positive ambition.

Use your apprenticeship to your advantage and discuss your design with your colleagues. Many will be keen to support you and to offer suggestions to help consolidate your aim and feedback on its narrative and representation. It is encouraged to learn from the expertise of your colleagues, but also to be tactical in who you ask for support and when you ask them. For instance, you could discuss your design with a technical specialist when choosing materials and developing construction details, or an environmental consultant when integrating and monitoring building performance and user comfort, or a conservation specialist when adapting or repurposing an existing building or working with a sensitive building fabric or context.

Beyond the access to human resources that you have available, you should also make the most of the physical resources in your practice, such as internal library resources (e-books, journal access, physical library), model-making workshops (materials, tools, equipment) and in-house CGI and illustration resources (software, licences, CPU power).

Many practices will have space to pin up work for internal reviews. Use this to your advantage also, and pin up your work to help structure your presentations and invite colleagues to review it. A great thing about presenting your design projects outside the university is that the review can happen more organically and does not need to follow an

Figure 3.34
Northumbria University,
Laura McClorey, Belfast
Stories. Sectional façade
model, demonstrating
elevation, material,
structure and space
all in one.

assessment format determined by your training provider.
This may help to relieve some pressure and be an
opportunity to test unique presentation techniques.
The Crit: An Architecture Student's Handbook[58] looks to
overturn the traditional crit and offers a range of playful
methods to review your work:

- role-play review
- introduction of real clients and users
- private view
- your work through the eyes of others
- roundtable meeting
- brochure review
- 'red dot' review
- double presentations.

There are countless ways you can benefit from your
practice to improve your design, communication and
narrative skills and to get inspired. However, you should also
invest time to explore creative activities and events outside
your practice, and those within and external to architecture.
These might include:

- end-of-year architecture shows
- awards shows:
  - RIBA President's Medals[59]
  - Architects for Health[60]

- Architecture MasterPrize[61]
- AJ Student Prize[62]
- architecture talks and podcasts
- workshops in photography, ceramics and life drawing, etc.
- online short courses (many universities provide free access to these resources for apprentices):
  - Udemy
  - LinkedIn Learning
  - EdX
  - Coursera.

Those you choose to attend will depend on your design sensibilities and creative interests. They are important opportunities to maintain your design skills but also to learn new ones. Design modules are an opportunity to explore innovative representational techniques and utilise cutting-edge technology and media to support your ideas. Digital technologies are likely to further embed into everyday practice working environments, and those who opt out only limit the services that they will be able to offer. Embracing novel methods to improve representation is an excellent way to demonstrate your commitment to lifelong learning and to showcase your design value in practice. Other areas related to technology to explore include:

- off-site manufacturing and construction
- 3D and 4D printing
- artificial intelligence and robotics
- generative modelling and visual coding
- building performance modelling
- Building Information Modelling (BIM)
- virtual reality (VR)
- augmented reality (AR)
- extended reality (XR).

Your practice may already have access to some of the software and hardware above, and by speaking to others you will meet colleagues who share the same passion for new technologies and potentially expand your own knowledge of what is possible.

Figure 3.35a and b (opposite) Sheffield Hallam University, Chris Jenkins, Fluid Lives. The Mirko lodges are inspired by the construction of traditional narrow boats and are contextualised within the Other Futures: Enabling Infrastructure brief as part of Design Studio 6 (Part 2 Winner, RIBA Yorkshire Student Awards 2023).

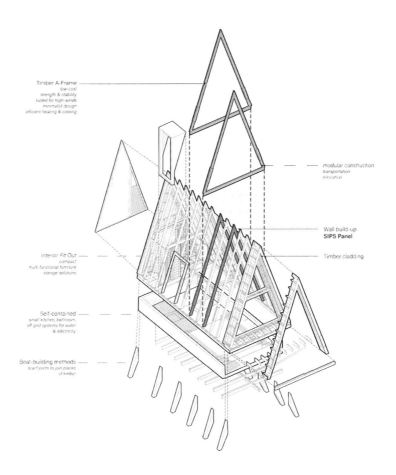

Timber A-Frame
low-cost
strength & stability
suited for high-winds
minimalist design
efficient heating & cooling

modular construction
transportation
relocation

Wall build-up
SIPS Panel

Timber cladding

Interior Fit Out
compact
multi-functional furniture
storage solutions

Self-contained
small kitchen, bathroom,
off-grid systems for water
& electricity

Boat-building methods
scarf joints to join planks
of timber

C9.
Building Conservation and Heritage

Cătălina Stroe is an apprentice at Peregrine Bryant Architects (PBA) and currently completing her Level 7 at the University of Bath. Cătălina outlines how an acute understanding of working with listed buildings in practice has informed her academic work on World Heritage Cities.

The apprenticeship course offered adaptability to focus on a relatable topic to the practice I am employed at. For the Environment and Sustainability course, my essay took a focus on building retrofit - a critical study about sustainable heating and water systems. My research specifically addressed stone buildings in Wales, developing knowledge for a current project in practice that involves a Grade II listed building, presently at Stage 2. The scope of the project aims to introduce air-source heat pumps and a 0% fossil fuel policy, determined by the client. Undertaking research during term time allowed me to enhance my knowledge and apply it on a live project at Peregrine Bryant.

My second year of the apprenticeship focused on World Heritage Cities. My essay compared Liverpool with Vienna, one city whose title has been revoked (Liverpool) and the other in danger of losing it. Although the topic focused on the future of World Heritage Cities, certain policies directly impact areas with listed buildings and interventions on them. For example, the World Heritage Committee iterated the need for historical buildings within the centre of Vienna to be preserved using traditional construction techniques, adhering to appropriate conservation needs. The city council applied the requested principles by organising a survey of all historical roofs in the centre to understand their current structural integrity and to devise techniques to provide better conservation strategies. The chance to integrate my professional interest within an academic context and to reapply it back into professional practice has proved the advantage of the apprenticeship.

Laura Morgante, Conservation Architect at Peregrine Bryant, outlines how the apprenticeship enabled Cătălina to complete her architectural education, whilst continuing to develop expertise in the practice:

Peregrine Bryant Architects is very pleased to support Cătălina through the apprenticeship scheme. It has given us the opportunity to support a valued young employee through the long and expensive architectural studies, ensuring the continuity of our relationship. It has given PBA the opportunity to guide Cătălina in studying topics that are of interest for our ongoing projects and development. It has been operationally challenging at times but has given Cătălina a true university experience, ensuring a continuity of full immersive university periods that Cătălina deserves.

Dr Rob Grover, Senior Lecturer and Director of Apprenticeship in Architecture, University of Bath, outlines how the apprenticeship has boosted Cătălina's exploration and develop designs aligned to her personal interests:

Cătălina used her apprenticeship training to examine the intersection of heritage and net zero building. This is a fundamental contemporary challenge, frequently framed as oppositional. Through using her Environmental and Sustainability essay to explore opportunities for low-carbon heating in vernacular Welsh architecture, she was directly able to translate this new knowledge to practice. This was enabled by the freedom of this aspect of the programme, in which apprentices can choose their own themes to research that build on, and extend, their practice experience.

Here are some suggested practice-based activities that might similarly help you understand the legislative framework and principals of conservation practice.

- Review Listed Building planning consents that your practice have submitted to review the level of information required.
- Review Heritage Statements on projects to learn more about the information included in these reports.
- Find out more about the RIBA Conservation register and its process.
- Speak to colleagues on the RIBA Conservation Architect register.
- Read up on the International Council on Monuments and Sites (ICOMOS) to understand the training guidelines and competences related to conservation.
- Speak to your employer and request time on a conservation or heritage project, if available.

RIBA CPD core curriculum content (available on RIBA Academy):

- **Heritage and Listed Buildings: Understanding the legislative framework for heritage and listed buildings** - understand who does what in historic building conservation in the UK and how architects can navigate structures and policies.
- **RIBA Professional Services Contract 2020: Conservation Architectural Services** - expand your knowledge on writing the Concise and Domestic Professional Services Contract 2020: Conservation and how the documents are structured.

Scan the QR code to visit the CPD page.

C10.
Design, Construction and Technology

Elizabeth Akamo is a second-year apprentice at Scott Brownrigg and Oxford Brookes University, working primarily in the residential and mixed-use sectors. Elizabeth's intrigue for spatial design and the study between bodies and space has matured her focus in human-centred architecture, applied through her university and practice work.

My academic work explores 'what makes a good city and what makes us want to come to the city'; it examines why we choose to stay in cities, socialise here, build our lives and futures in such complex contexts. The aim is to understand how cities can be designed so that they are places we want to live, without feeling as though we are compromising on our quality of life. University has supported my passion to investigate human-centred design in-depth and develop an open and collaborative mind in the process.

Professional practice has furthered my architectural knowledge and skills through engagement with live projects that are directly transferable to my academic work. I recently concluded working on a master planning project that influenced decisions on my academic work, understanding how to investigate possible multiple sites for intervention.

The great thing about the apprenticeship is that I can tailor my professional development around specific interests, particularly working in the residential and mixed-use sector. As I collaborate on the design of dwellings and community space, I simultaneously explore these ideas in a variety of ways through my academic work.

When Elizabeth is not focusing on her university project, she seeks out ways to continue her education, whether through CPDs activities, talks, learning from colleagues with specialist knowledge or simply more informal conversation in the office. The practice environment is an enabler of dialogue and the sharing of ideas. She adds:

The hybrid learning structure of the apprenticeship is helping me to refine my multitasking skills, forcing me to think critically and holistically about numerous aspects of a design. I am confident that this facilitates more creative design solutions, as I gain more professional experience on projects and progress in my career.

Matthew Humphreys, Associate at Scott Borwnrigg, and Elizabeth's mentor comments on the effectiveness of Elizabeth's communication skills and engagement within project teams:

Supporting the next generation of architects is crucial for the future success of Scott Brownrigg, and the wider profession. At Scott Brownrigg we are proud to have been pivotal within the Architecture Apprenticeships Trailblazer Group to set up the architecture apprenticeship scheme and we are keen to continue to provide alternative routes into the profession.

Elizabeth has had a significant impact on the practice and her inquisitive nature has forced project leaders to question decisions and standard practices to achieve a considered,

Figure 3.36 Oxford Brookes University, Elizabeth Akamo, The Good City: Future-proofing cities through human-centred design. Sketches and diagrams help to inform design decisions that later will result in construction. Understanding massing, layout and orientation are all key to get right from the outset and will determine the success of the project later.

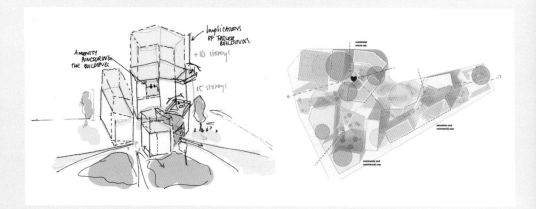

Figure 3.37 Scott Brownrigg, Maker's Yard. A new mixed commercial and residential use development on a brownfield site adjacent to the canal. The project design adopted the council's Climate Emergency Action Plan and a fabric-first approach.

progressive output. Furthermore, her academic research has a direct relationship with projects on the drawing board, which has helped inform and add credibility to design decisions.

Elizabeth's tutor **Denis Vlieghe at Oxford Brookes University** discusses Elizabeth's academic journey and the benefits of the apprenticeship as a reciprocal learning environment:

Elizabeth joined the Oxford Brookes Apprenticeships Programme in September 2021 with focus on collaborative research and knowledge exchange with industry. Throughout her academic development, she demonstrated an exemplary attitude when faced with new learning challenges. She has been involved in our partnership with Homes England and OPDC [Old Oak and Park Royal], discussing design solutions for the delivery of quality homes for the Old Oak and Park Royal redevelopment together with project stakeholders. This experience, along with her training, had a positive impact on her approach within the housing team at the office. She approaches her work with a critical mindset helping her progress both in academia and professional practice.

Here are some suggested practice-based activities that might similarly help you understand and keep up-to-date with technical, design, engineering, services and technological issues, trends and changes.

- Work closely with a project architect to understand techniques for design brief development and refinement.
- Review project planning documents for submissions of different scale and complexity. This will help identify the number of stakeholders and their roles.
- Engage in specification writing and material selection on a project.
- Participate in manufacturer and factory visits to understand more about how materials and products are made and procured.
- Get on site as much as you can to learn more about the processes involved at construction stages.
- Request Building Information Modelling (BIM) training as part of your annual review if not already complete.

RIBA CPD core curriculum content (available on RIBA Academy):

- **Building regulations essentials: principles, requirements and specification for fire safety –** learn more about the planned regulatory changes to Approved Document Part B to ensure compliance.
- **Innovation in Technology series –** explore the opportunities and challenges of integrating new technology into architectural practice, such as artificial intelligence and big data.

Scan the QR code to visit the CPD page.

E6.

Business Skills

RIBA Business Skills focuses on 'developing capability in business skills relevant to working in practice and practice management'.[63] This is oriented towards emerging professionals with the ambition to work in and eventually lead architectural practice, and for those keen to develop innovative approaches to the business of architecture.

At a glance:

- **KSBs:** K6, S6, K7, S7, K10, S10, S12, K13, S13, K15, S15, K16, S16 & B1–B7
- **RIBA CPD core curriculum:** This Theme and Value for Architectural Education is not attributed to any of the 10 RIBA CPD criteria. However, it can be found across the entirety of the core curriculum and in the other Themes and Values.

Expert perspective
by Tim Bell, Melissa Dowler and Hari Phillips

Tim Bell, Melissa Dowler and Hari Phillips are Directors at Bell Phillips Architects, based in London. They discuss why business skills are an essential for any emerging professional and why client relationships, employee satisfaction and self-promotion are key to business longevity and success.

An understanding of the commercial aspects of running a practice is vital in becoming a productive and efficient member of an architectural team. Apprentices who work on bid submissions, attend client meetings and understand project costs and profitability develop a commercial understanding of the business which is crucial when operating in a competitive market. If apprentices can gain basic knowledge of fees, grade rates, resourcing and profit margins, they will begin to understand the importance of efficiency, time management and business development. If this is coupled with transparency from an organisation relating to its financial opportunities and challenges, then apprentices attuned to these commercial aspects become more valuable members of the team.

At Bell Phillips we believe that apprentices develop key business skills during their work in practice which those studying via the traditional route may not be exposed to. Apprentices learn the scope of work for each project so that they can identify requests from clients outside the brief and fee agreement. In uncertain times, with many projects delayed or subject to a change of brief, it is essential that

Figure 3.38a and b
Bell Phillips Architects, The Tree House, Southwark. The project involved working closely with the client and local authority to design and construct a community pavilion within a new park.

additional or prolongation fees are requested to ensure the viability of the project. Working with senior staff and attending meetings affords apprentices an enhanced appreciation of client management which, in-turn, builds client relationship skills that are vital to business development and their future careers.

In the office, working groups review issues such as future technologies, BIM, sustainability, graphical standards, social value, post-occupancy evaluation, new business development and emerging policy. All apprentices are invited to join at least one working group to start to develop their specialisms, which will be key in their future career. These groups also provide a mechanism for future-proofing the business, making sure we are at the forefront of new ways of working.

The skills required to manage and maintain a successful business are in constant flux, requiring practices to periodically review and reassess the unique skills that they can offer to remain competitive and relevant. Challenging economic circumstances have made business agility and resilience planning more necessary than ever. Therefore, those able to understand the needs of contemporary practice and its management, and able to uphold the values of architectural practice, will be an asset to any employer. Business skills developed in university can take many forms and might be integrated into any number of modules. Module assessments that challenge your business skills may require you to:

- write a business plan
- benchmark (your employer's) competitors and strategise to find new work
- write bids and manage project fees
- source new clients and manage relationships at different stages and during difficult scenarios.

As an apprentice, you can benefit from the resources offered by your employer to enhance your knowledge of running a business. Whether your employer is a large practice or a sole practitioner, it will have information to support your learning. This might be in the form of templates (letters, programmes and specifications), previous project documentation (planning sets, Design and Access Statements and record sets) and project administration (variation letters, requests for information and stage checklists).

Santiago Wagner Velez, apprentice at University of Nottingham and AHMM, one of the largest employers of qualified architects in the UK, which means that Santiago has an extensive knowledge base to learn from. AHMM is an employee-owned business and a member of the Employee Ownership Association,[64] which means that Santiago can also learn more about emerging architectural practice types and compare against more traditional forms such as sole practitioner, Partnership, LLP, LTP and PLC. Santiago discusses how his design thesis identified post-occupancy evaluations as an opportunity for the practice to offer a greater level of services for clients and users:

The apprenticeship allowed me to develop knowledge in school design through a research study with narrative analysis for a recently completed project. AHMM supported me with access to their vast knowledge of school design and interview catalogues. This knowledge will inform my future practice in the design of learning spaces and through social, value-led post-occupancy evaluations (POE), a developing area for architects to measure the performance of their buildings once in use.

Santiago benefits from the reciprocity between academia and practice, using recent projects to help inform his research methods in university. Furthermore, the skills to conduct POEs on educational buildings is opportune for AHMM's knowledge of the design of future educational projects.

There are ample opportunities for employer and training provider reciprocity to assess business skills. These might develop as co-created briefs, specialist lectures and site visits. For example, co-created assessments might require:

- Development of an outline fee proposal for a new project that your employer is bidding for, considering fees, programme and resourcing.
- Strategising methods to manage and sustain your practice during economic downturn (recession), based on your employer's current workload. Thinking about project count and timelines, employee work schedules, business overheads and innovative approaches to income generation.
- Discussing the impact of technology to keep your employer agile. How could you measure performance and efficiencies of these technologies? How might it be translated into research and development?

Mark Kemp's *Good Practice Guide: Business Resilience* (2022)[65] identifies **organisation** and **people** as two key areas that all businesses must have a handle on to remain resilient. Kemp divides these headings into practice, projects, providers and staff, clients and consultants. All businesses require a clear strategy of delivery to focus, measure and meet their targets. A good exercise for you is to review whether your employer can clearly articulate their position on each of these bullet points:

- business strategy for delivery
- business plan
- what you want to do
- how you want to do it
- how you are going to be successful at it
- clear sense of purpose and direction.

Until recently, employers have tended to focus on delivering projects suited to their practice profile, offering a range of architectural services. However, more recently, employers recognise the benefit of interdisciplinary teams to help deliver projects and increase the services that they can offer to clients, such as environmental engineering, sustainability, material research, industrial design, UX/UI (user experience/user interface), graphic design and model-making. Specialist appointments to diversify a team might include computer scientists, physicians, engineers and even philosophers!

Being able to work with and communicate with others is inherent in procuring new work. RIBA's *Business Resilience Roadmap*[66] presents three sections as guides to help architects to succeed in matters relating to strategy and winning work, practice culture, and fees and finance. The roadmap is an accessible starting point if you are considering starting your own practice and need to find work. It also provides opportunities for student members to improve their business skills and knowledge. Some other key resources related to business skills are:

- RIBA Future Leaders annual programme
- '12 Golden rules: The importance of having a written form of appointment'[67]
- *How To Win Work: The architect's guide to business development and marketing*[68]
- *Starting a Practice: A Plan of Work*[69]
- *Handbook of Practice Management 10th edition*[70]

For practices to remain relevant, they must keep up-to-date with the work and running of other businesses in the profession. It is critical for employers to benchmark against other architectural offices. This is also a useful exercise for you to understand how your employer compares to its competitors and understand key trends in the profession.

Top tip for benchmarking

Benchmarking can help you identify the direction of travel of the profession. It can assist you in understanding areas of strength and weakness, and performance. It also provides useful insight into staff numbers and salaries across Chartered Practices, helping you to locate your own salary within this. It also presents data on non-financial areas such as EDI (Equity, Diversity and Inclusion) and workloads, all of which might inform your future moves.

In 2022, there were 3,577 RIBA Chartered Practices in the UK. Of these, 2,058 practices were either sole practitioners or employed under five members of staff, whilst there were 45 practices employing more than 100 staff.[71] Whatever your ambitions (large, medium or small employer), it is worth noting that larger employers typically have the resource capacity to manage a larger portfolio of projects, as well as the time to generate international work. This might open opportunities to work on a range of large-scale or mixed-use projects, and the chance to work abroad after your apprenticeship. Other important business skills to help you get ahead include:

- supervising the work of others
- process of controlling building costs
- meeting the client's brief within the constraints and imposed budget and building regulations
- marketing and promoting the practice
- financial management
- embedding research into practice
- understanding the importance of fair remuneration for professional services
- monitoring and complying with fair remuneration for staff and staff salaries.

The following case studies present two examples where apprentices have developed management skills related to running architectural practice and sustaining business. Experience with client relationships and negotiation, teamworking, planning and scope of services are discussed – all of which are key skills for an emerging professional.

Business Skills 1
Clients and consultants

Oliver Howard is an Architect at Coleman Anderson Architects, who specialise in bespoke residential architecture. Oliver completed his apprenticeship at London South Bank University and discusses the opportunities of working in a small practice, his exposure to clients and consultant teams and shadowing the practice's Managing Director.

The apprenticeship was a necessary and convenient route to completing my architectural training. I had been keen to return to my RIBA Parts 2 and 3 studies for a couple of years prior to learning about apprenticeships. However, the high cost of traditional postgraduate studies was a big deterrent to me applying. Once on the course, I was drawn to modules focused on developing skills related to sustainable architecture and was encouraged to research precedents found in nature. The modules centred on a theme of 're-wilding', which is a growing environmental and social agenda in the UK, and one I hope will keep momentum. I was able to transfer knowledge from the modules at university into my practice work, developing an architectural language that sought to enhance biodiversity and the ecology of a site. I learnt to develop project briefs and identify clients and users for my university work and have applied these skills when working with clients in practice. The Part 3 activities on my apprenticeship introduced the legal and regulatory issues architects must adhere to, along with procurement techniques, client management and business running. I am fortunate to be working in a small practice and have gained valuable exposure across RIBA Work Stages 4, 5 and 6, and work to apply the sustainability strategy to the projects I am working on. This real-world experience has helped me to contextualise the themes covered in university and to apply them in the office.

Figure 3.39 London South Bank University, Oliver Howard, Soma. The project focused on promoting the medicinal value of wildflowers in Britain. The herb-drying Soma store allows visitors to exchange plants and herbs for their dry weight to use for medicine.

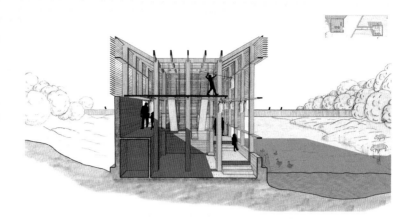

It has also allowed me to develop my professional skills and to identify ways in which the practice can improve our processes and systems related to running a sustainable business.

I continued to develop the KSBs gained during the apprenticeship within the residential sector where a large majority of design decisions are driven by the client's aspiration and their budget. Whilst studying within a university setting may be considered hyperbolic compared with real-world design, I continue to explore ways of breaking boundaries between 'natural ecosystems' and the perceived antonym of the human environment, whilst simultaneously managing our client aspirations. I am an advocate for continued professional development and believe that the new mandatory requirements are a necessary step to rebuilding trust between clients and users. The better we can integrate study and practice, the more potential there is for meaningful collaboration, which can boost our marketing, reach new clients, generate new business and enable bids for new funding routes.

Stuart Coleman, Managing Director at Coleman Anderson, provides comment on how the apprenticeship has supported the business's agility, with reciprocity through real-world experiences and communication skills:

Employing architectural assistants within the practice and encouraging them to pursue the apprenticeship course has been extremely beneficial. Their experience within the practice helps inform the projects being realised at university; this is reciprocated in their development of technological advancements that they bring back to the practice. Moreover, we can provide a support structure which is often lacking to individuals studying full time. Through the apprenticeship scheme we can foster a commitment to architecture; ultimately this is an investment in talented individuals that enhances our practice and the profession.

Business Skills 2
Teamwork and collaboration

Eleanor Lee is an apprentice at the University of Cambridge and GSSArchitecture. Eleanor outlines how group modules that form part of the residency structure of the course at Cambridge have developed her teamworking and communication skills, and how she is able to apply these into practice.

I chose the University of Cambridge's apprenticeship course because of its flexibility and emphasis on targeting skills directly linked to professional practice through intensive teamwork design modules. Specifically, the Teamwork module includes focused lectures on effective teamworking and tasks a critical reflection piece on collaborative working and its effects on professional performance. Rather than being focused on an individual's development, as many full-time courses might be, the structure requires small group collaborative working and the sharing of reflections on our practical experiences.

Applied in group design tasks, the challenge of most modules is to learn, absorb, design, iterate and deliver on a specific area of the industry within an intensive two-week residential. For example, one module runs as a masterclass on *Façade Design, taught by a range of engineers, product specialists, researchers and architects, such that a spectrum of perspectives informs the design response. Methodologies of intense group working are carried across to live projects, allowing me to demonstrate communication, organisation and coordination skills, developing greater understanding of the players within design teams. Testing ideas through these Design Challenges enables an increased confidence and provides fresh perspectives to studio design reviews and challenges innovation. Simultaneously, progressing academically and in practice enriches my day-to-day activities, providing an invaluable, accelerated career trajectory. As such, the practice has recently felt such confidence in my progress that I'm taking a lead role on a mid-sized refurbishment project based in Yorkshire.*

These focused modules have allowed me to pursue my research curiosities, that then filter into practice. The Façade Design module illuminated a strategy for working through details that I've since applied to a project at RIBA Stages 4 and 5 and recently completed on site. Sustainability-driven modules have encouraged me to become a champion within the practice, a member of our sustainability steering group, and I am currently undertaking training to become a SKA Assessor.[72] I aim to continue to gain exposure to a range of projects that we take on in the practice that can only bolster my career.

Alex Proctor, Senior Associate at GSSArchitecture, highlights the reciprocity between university and practice and how Eleanor has embraced this opportunity through the programming and management of her design projects:

Our experience of the Cambridge apprenticeship course has been extremely positive, which is primarily due to the clear, consistent lines of communication. The subject matter taught at Cambridge aligns well with themes GSSArchitecture is exploring in practice, such as carbon reduction in the built environment. Eleanor is part of our sustainability steering group, contributing towards research and resources used practice wide. Cambridge's two-week

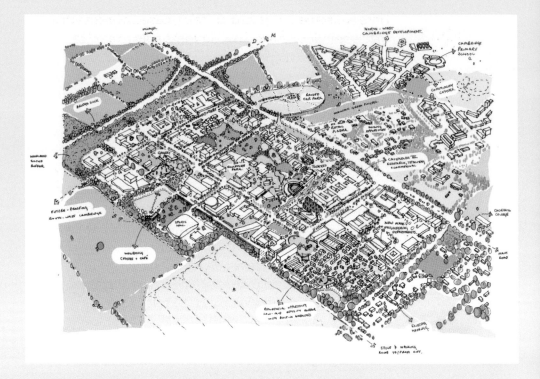

residential model works better for us than the day-release equivalent in some respects. Eleanor's time at university is approached much like annual leave, with handovers to colleagues, and the flexibility of her study leave enables her studies to work alongside project demands well.

Dr Timothy Brittain-Catlin is Eleanor's tutor at the **University of Cambridge**. Timothy outlines Eleanor's collaborative skills and notes how important this is when developing fundamental business skills:

Eleanor has been an exemplary apprentice. She is very quick to grasp the professional potential of every situation both on the course and in practice and therefore has been able to combine the two effectively. Apprentices are, generally, well organised when scheduling work and training commitments because their office practice requires them to be so. We can see this for example in the contributions she made to our teamworking and collaborative skills module and through the responses of her mentor.

Figure 3.40 University of Cambridge, Eleanor Lee, Module 2 Working in Teams, MSt Year 1. Group work project masterplan involving the analysis of an existing area and understanding potential clients and needs.

Here are some suggested practice-based activities that might help you develop key business skills related to running and managing a practice.

- Engage in projects at strategic brief, understanding management of client aspirations and creating fee proposals.
- Review letters of appointment and scope of services to understand how to formalise an agreement for work.
- Understand how your employer manages their book-keeping and the systems that are in place to do this.
- Discuss your practice's strategy for forecasting fees and resourcing.
- Set your own business plan, considering how you would like your practice to develop in the next five years.
- Find out about your employer's Professional Indemnity Insurance and what it covers.
- Speak to senior colleagues to understand more about managing teams and how they are budgeted.

Beyond the resources available on the RIBA Academy, there are many other resources to enhance your business skills. These are found in and outside of architecture. Here are some suggestions for you:

- Institute of Directors[73]
- Federation of Small Businesses[74]
- Chambers of Commerce[75]
- *Good Practice Guide: Business Resilience*[76]
- *Good Practice Guide: Professionalism at Work*[77]
- *Good Practice Guide: Fees.*[78]

Part 3

The Part 3 curriculum will be delivered by either your training provider or in partnership with the RIBA for those without a Part 3 validated course. Typically, the format is one of a postgraduate certificate, postgraduate diploma or advanced diploma. For the purpose of professional qualification, it is inconsequential which of these you obtain.

The Part 3 curriculum is principally concerned with the Professional Criteria which are held in common by the RIBA and the ARB. These are summarised in the following subject headings:

- Professionalism (K12, S12)
- Clients, user and delivery of services (K13, S13)
- Legal framework and processes (K14, S14)
- Practice and management (K15, S15)
- Building procurement (K16, S16).

Whilst traditionally referred to as PC1 to PC5, they have different abbreviations within the apprenticeship, as they essentially follow on from the knowledge and skills at Part 2. The delivery and teaching of these will likely employ a combination of the following methods:

- lectures
- seminars
- one-to-one/small group tutorials
- scenarios-based/role-playing workshops
- webinars
- online study packs.

Top tip for peer-to-peer support

There is a long tradition of Part 3 candidates, including most recently apprentices, choosing to form peer support groups. These groups, increasingly facilitated via remote communication platforms, come together between structured learning sessions to consolidate and enhance their understanding, work through problems together and help one another to stay on track. We recommend that you form one from the outset of your Part 3 course.

Similarly, depending on your course, you will be likely to be assessed through a combination of the following methods:

- written assignments
- office-based scenario questions (open-book examination)
- oral examination
- CV
- PEDR log sheets.

In addition to meeting the ARB Professional Criteria, the RIBA expects Part 3 candidates to be able to demonstrate evidence of their understanding of relevant subject materials applied in practice, as follows and as illustrated through the preceding apprentice case studies:[79]

1. Architecture for social purpose.
2. Health, safety and wellbeing.
3. Business, clients and services.
4. Legal, regulatory and statutory compliance.
5. Procurement and contracts.
6. Sustainable architecture.
7. Inclusive environments.
8. Places, planning and communities.
9. Building conservation and heritage.
10. Design, construction and technology.

As an apprentice, likely with a minimum of four to five years of professional practical experience, you are especially well placed to evidence these subject matters and further consolidate them through the structured learning at Part 3.

Expert perspective
by Professor Stephen Brookhouse

Professor Stephen Brookhouse, author of *Part 3 Handbook*,[80] acknowledges the strengths of apprentice candidates but equally warns of typical pitfalls:

Architecture is a practice-based profession. The apprenticeship route – with its blend of experiential learning in the 'studio' and in 'practice' – definitely gives students an 'edge' in developing a deeper understanding of practice and the behaviours required to succeed as an architect.

Tutoring apprentices on their practice-based coursework, I often see a good practical knowledge of the immediate issues in the design and delivery of the projects they are working on. There is a danger, though, that this depth of practical knowledge is at the expense of an understanding of the wider context of practice and professional standards that go beyond their immediate experience.

What is often missing is the knowledge and understanding of different ways of practising architecture and the wider – perhaps more conceptual – approaches to issues such as project risk, professional ethics and alternative and more innovative ways of delivering projects.

Experience is not everything and practitioners and mentors are not always good at articulating the issues that practice faces both in the day-to-day and long term. So, students need to find that 'place' – both mentally and physically – to think objectively about their experiences in an informed way.

I find that my role, increasingly, is to facilitate students' reflection: to widen horizons to offer insights into practice and to encourage dialogue in the office, with other students and tutoring staff.

Ultimately, students need to develop the skills for ethical future practice: to be a key actor in an increasingly challenging world of project design and delivery – that is where our current and future value lies as professional architects.

Stephen has also kindly provided the following 'top tips' to assist you with your Part 3 studies:

- Use your workplace as a key resource for critical thinking about practice.
- Engage with your mentor and colleagues – there are always alternative views and insights to be gained.
- Focus on your own approach to ethical professional behaviour: 'How would I deal with this...?' as much as the baseline competence to complete a project task.
- Challenge your specific experiences by placing them in the wider context of practice.
- Challenge office practice and make positive critical points about your current experiences.
- Learn to reflect using your wider professional knowledge to inform your understanding.
- Use every opportunity to consider and propose 'better future practice' based on your reflections.

End Point Assessment (EPA)

The EPA is the final stage of your architecture apprenticeship. It is an impartial assessment intended to determine whether you have developed the KSBs outlined in the Architecture Apprenticeship Standard. In a way, it is a test of readiness to practice.

The EPA gateway

Prior to taking the EPA, you need to meet certain prerequisites. The following checklist will help you and your employer determine whether you are eligible:

- Achieved Level 2 English and maths (sometimes referred to as functional skills).
- Completed and awarded a Part 2 qualification.
- Successfully completed all Part 3 learning and assessments (outwith the EPA).
- Completed any formal Training Plan agreed with your employer.
- Display the KSBs as defined in the Architecture Apprenticeship Standard.

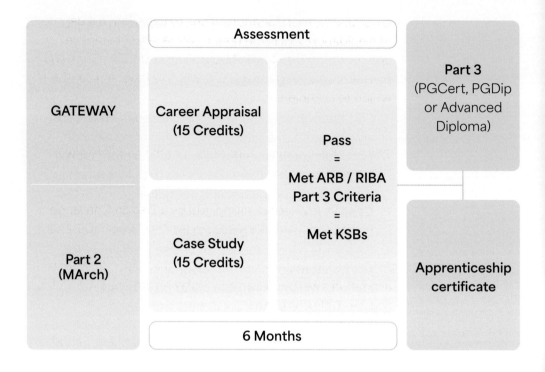

Figure 3.41 The relationship between gateway and EPA.

To help determine whether apprentices have met these gateway requirements, some training providers ask apprentices to collate an evidential portfolio. If this is asked of you, the following content may act as a guide:

- Studio design projects (including development work) and accompanying reports.
- Taught module submissions (e.g. written examination scripts, essays and dissertation).
- Completed PEDR log sheets.
- Progress review meeting records.
- CPD certificates.
- Sample of work-based project work.
- OTJ (off-the-job) training logs.
- Mapping overview of apprentice progress and learning against KSBs.

Whilst they may consult your training provider, it is ultimately your employer who will decide whether to put you forward for the EPA. They should also afford you an opportunity to express your views on whether you feel ready to pass through the gateway. Whilst it is not uncommon for apprentices to experience a degree of trepidation, this is the time to voice any substantive concerns you may have about taking your EPA. Once you pass through the gateway, you will only have six months in which to complete it.

The EPA

The EPA takes a maximum of six months and comprises two assessment methods:

1. Case Study Report supported by a Design Challenge.
2. Professional Interview supported by Career Appraisal.

As the EPA comprises 30 credits of the overall Part 3 credit allocation, the Part 3 can only be awarded once the EPA is satisfactorily completed.

Whilst the traditional Case Study Report and Professional Interview are comprehensively discussed in the invaluable RIBA-approved *Part 3 Handbook,*[81] it is worth highlighting some of the nuances of these assessments within the context of your apprenticeship.

Case Study Report supported by a Design Challenge

As an apprentice, you will be required to undertake a Design Challenge in your workplace after the EPA gateway. It involves the practical application of creative problem-solving and professional management, and allows you to demonstrate the 13 KSBs being assessed (see Appendix A). The Design Challenge is somewhat contentious, not least because it appears to be an additional assessment component over and above that required of the traditional route. In reality, the Case Study Report – of which the Design Challenge forms part – is largely the same as a conventional Part 3 case study. The main difference is that the EPA Case Study Report, in being mapped to the KSBs of the Architecture Apprenticeship Standard, requires evidence against select Part 2 criteria, opposed to solely those at Part 3.

You, your employer and EPAO will need to agree the subject of the Design Challenge within four weeks of the EPA start date. It is important to bear in mind that it must be of a sufficient scale and complexity to enable the practical demonstration of the necessary KSBs. The Design Challenge may relate to either the whole or part of a real-life project.[82]

Further, it must be achievable within the five-to-six-month timescale. Remember it is undertaken wholly in your workplace; you will no longer receive the 20% off-the-job training allocation.[83]

Additionally, it must allow you to:[84]

- Utilise a variety of analogue and digital techniques.
- Demonstrate the integration of structural principles and construction techniques with a building design (e.g. structural coordination).
- Demonstrate an understanding of national and/or local planning processes and assessment of the impact of development on the local context and environment.
- Analyse, prioritise and respond to a brief and other client requirements.
- Demonstrate competence in the evaluation, selection and integration of suitable materials and technologies.
- Demonstrate the application of legal, contractual and regulatory compliance and financial control.
- Demonstrate application of creative problem-solving and professional management in practice.
- Analyse and respond to a project management and contract scenario.
- Demonstrate competence in dealing professionally with project challenges and complexities.

The Case Study Report should include the following:[85]

1. **Introduction** - outline details of the practice you work in and your role.
2. **Definition of the task** - outline the Design Challenge and its physical and contractual context and any constraints.
3. **Description** - of the processes utilised to manage and

deliver the Design Challenge. This might include explored design options, participatory workshops or value engineering exercises. Identify and explain the role of colleagues or specialist consultants to the design development.

4. **KSBs** – describe how the relevant KSBs are met and demonstrated (see Figures 3.43 and 3.44).

5. **Examples** – include examples of work undertaken during the Design Challenge. This will likely include a selection of text, diagrams, drawings or digital models, specifications, schedules, visualisations, photographs and/or physical models. Note that all sections must include at least one illustration (see Figures 3.43 and 3.44).

6. **Conclusion** – reflective appraisal of the processes and an explanation of how the output met the Design Challenge brief.

Overall, the Case Study Report, including the Design Challenge component, should:[86]

- Be 10,000 words (+/-10% tolerance), excluding any appendices. The word count is higher than a conventional Part 3 case study because of the need to explain how the necessary KSBs have been met through the Design Challenge. This may either be interspersed within or appended to the Case Study Report.

- Be submitted in electronic format (PDF) to the End Point Assessment Organisation (EPAO) within six months of the EPA start date.

- Be accompanied by confirmation from your employer that the report submitted is your own work and that your claim of your contributions to the project is accurate.

Your Case Study Report will be marked by an Independent Assessor and Industry Expert, appointed by the EPAO, neither of whom will have any previous experience of you. Some apprentices and employers have found it difficult to grasp what is required of the Design Challenge and harder still to locate examples. To assist, we have produced abstracts of two Design Challenge examples submitted by the first cohort of architecture apprentices nationally:

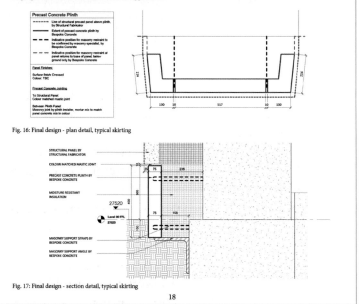

4.0 Construction

The final agreed solution, which is approved for construction but yet to be installed on site, is a hybrid of previous iterations and looks to form the skirtings using precast concrete, per Option Three, but in unitised form, like Option Two. The use of precast concrete marries with the elevational design while the block sized pieces allow safe manual handling and installation. Fig. 16 shows the technical design of a typical skirting. A stainless steel angle fixed to the slab edge provides a shelf off which the blocks are built (Fig. 17). The option to construct the skirtings off the foundations was dismissed, as the top of found height varies around the building by up to 800mm, meaning the skirtings would need to extend to a range of depths, thus preventing standardisation. The skirting blocks are tied to the slab edge using steel restraint straps, in a manner similar to the way ashlar stone is fixed to a backing substrate. Mortar jointing between the blocks is colour-coded to the concrete, helping to create the desired monolithic appearance.

Insulation fitted behind the units is required to be both moisture and fire resistant. With limited options available on the market that meet these dual performance requirements, an expensive Foamglas product was chosen, though costs were mitigated through material optimisation and standardisation of the thicknesses required (Fig. 18 overleaf).

4.1 Knowledge, skills and behaviours

The process of arriving at the finalised design, with due consideration given to cost, buildability and future maintenance requirements, satisfies many of the apprenticeship's key attributes, including Knowledge and Skills criteria 1 (design), 6 (the role of the architect), 8-13 (construction matters, cost, statutory compliance, ideation, and management of client relations) and 15-16 (team working, record keeping and collaboration), along with Behaviours 1-5 (integrity and objectivity). For an extended summary, refer to Appendix A.

Fig. 16: Final design - plan detail, typical skirting

Fig. 17: Final design - section detail, typical skirting

18

Figure 3.42 Select page from Design Challenge Example No. 1.
Discussion of the final skirting panel design, accompanied by typical plan and section technical details, and learning reflections against associated KSBs.

Design Challenge Example No. 1

An apprentice with many years' experience is responsible for the delivery of a 30,000sq m mixed-use office and retail scheme. The case study starts with an introduction to the project, and their role and involvement. The study then describes the project through the following RIBA Plan of Work stages: project environment (0-2); legal framework (2-3); procurement, contract choice and tendering (4-5); and manufacturing and construction (5-6).

As the apprentice assumes an unusually high level of responsibility, it was necessary for them to identify a discrete Design Challenge in their case study project.

They choose to focus on the design and buildability challenges encountered in the detailing of a skirting panel to be installed to the base of a ground-floor colonnade.

They start by describing the challenge – the need to protect against low-level splashback and staining from ground moisture, existing construction programme and sequencing constraints, cost and fabrication efficiencies, and fire safety requirements. The apprentice then describes how the challenge was overcome through the design process; for example, analysing building precedents with similar components, sketching and digital modelling of material assembly options in collaboration with the façade specialist, and consulting building control and a fire engineer.

Design Challenge Example No. 2

An apprentice is working on the redevelopment of a Grade II listed building, a former pattern shop. The case study starts with an introduction to the project, and their role and involvement. The study then describes the project through the following RIBA Plan of Work stages: project environment (0-2); legal framework (2-3); procurement, contract choice and tendering (4-5); and manufacturing and construction (5-6).

While working on the project, the apprentice was tasked with redesigning the south elevation in response to successive value engineering exercises throughout the duration of the project, providing a suitably scaled and complex Design Challenge. They start by describing the challenge – the brief for the undercroft and adjacent public realm, including the original sustainability and biodiversity aspirations and master planning strategies, conservation constraints, and cost control and budget limitations. The apprentice then describes how the challenge was resolved through the design process; for example, the effective use of visual aids to enable client understanding and decision-making on the retention, substitution or removal of select elements, precedents research for the rainscreen cladding, evaluation of possible materials and techniques including waste reduction measures, and the coordination of architectural and structural information.

VALUE ENGINEERING: STEEL FRAMING SYSTEM / EXISTING BLOCKWORK

Fig 05 highlights the initial vision of what was possible for the Pattern Shop re-development particularly including the south elevation public realm. The initial client budget was £1.5 million. It was identified early in the project that the current condition of the building required extensive stabilisation work which would require most of the current available budget. Therefore, whilst the client looked for further funding avenues it was agreed that reducing the glazing to the south elevation would assist in reducing costs. The elevation was subsequently revised to reduce the glazing to 3 curtain walling panels (Fig 06).

The original intention was for the south elevation to have the existing blockwork (Fig 07) wall demolished and to be rebuilt as an SFS system with curtain wall glazing elements. One of the value engineering exercises which took place was an exploration into the possibility of retaining the existing blockwork wall and forming openings for the curtain walling within this to reduce the quantity of steel required to be purchased and installed. It was proposed by the Quantity Surveyor that retaining the blockwork wall could save in circa £55,000 and was therefore accepted by the client. This then resulted in a series of discussions occurring between ourselves and the structural engineer as to how best approach retaining the wall, the outcome of which is discussed within the detailed design chapter.

KSB6 - Role of the Architect
This exercise demonstrated this skill by beginning to explore and make decisions as to how to best approach development of the south elevation through retaining the blockwork whilst also taking a lead in developing this with the structural engineer.

KSB10 - Finance and Regulation
This skill was demonstrated by being part of the process to control the building cost and budget limitations whilst still working to meet the clients' requirements and brief.

Professional Interview supported by Career Appraisal

As is the case with the traditional route, you will be required to prepare a Career Appraisal based on your academic and professional practical experiences prior to the EPA gateway and mapped to the KSBs.

Following submission of the Career Appraisal, you will be required to attend a Professional Interview with the same two independent assessors. The interview will test your ability to evaluate, communicate and reflect on how the KSBs have been met and applied through your experiences, and your ability to learn from them. Ultimately, the purpose of the interview is to ascertain that you have the competence to work as an architect. In addition to the two independent assessors, the interview will be observed by a third person for the purpose of external quality assurance.[87] Their role is to ensure that it is fair, consistent and robust, so you need not worry about their presence; they are more concerned with the overall process than the performance of individual apprentices.

The Career Appraisal should refer to your academic and professional practical experience to demonstrate how each of the KSBs allocated to this assessment method

Figure 3.43 Select spreads from Design Challenge Example No. 2. Discussion of the impact of value engineering to the project, accompanied by a comparison of the original CGI and revised south elevation, and learning reflections against associated KSBs.

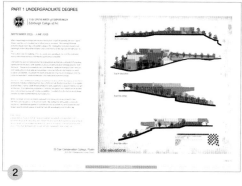

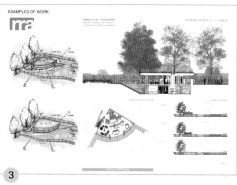

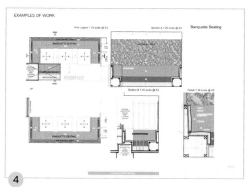

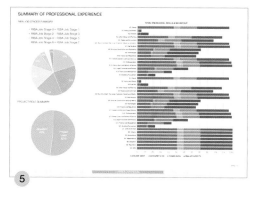

Figure 3.44 Typical
Career Appraisal.
Note the structure,
format and contents.

have been met and applied (see Appendix A). The appraisal
should cover your: [88]

- introduction to the profession 1
- academic experience at Part 1, Part 2 and Part 3 2
- professional practical experience 3
- current role and project work 4
- self-evaluation analysis 5
- career strengths and areas for improvement
- any emerging or specialist career interests
- career professional development strategy.

The document should be provided as narrative text, presenting your academic and professional career in a coherent and engaging way. As the appraisal is intended to be critically reflective, you will need to write in the first person (singular and plural). Each event will invariably be illustrated and descriptively annotated. Each section should explain how any relevant KSBs have been met and applied (see Appendix A).

The Career Appraisal should be:[89]

- 4,000 words (+/-10% tolerance)
- submitted in electronic format (PDF) to the EPAO within six months of the EPA start date and in advance of the Professional Interview
- accompanied by confirmation from your employer that all evidence submitted is your own work.

As the experience included within the Career Appraisal is completed prior to the EPA gateway, only the Professional Interview will be marked and contribute to the End Point Assessment.

The Professional Interview requirements are outlined as follows:[90]

- It is based wholly on the Career Appraisal and should demonstrate clearly how you have met the required KSBs (see Appendix A).
- As such, all questions posed by the panel will be based on your Career Appraisal. The questions are agreed in advance by the two independent assessors and offer all parties an opportunity to clarify any ambiguity about how you have met certain KSBs as outlined in the Career Appraisal.
- As the Career Appraisal itself is not graded, the panel will also need to explore the level of your occupational competence.
- It will take place within the final two weeks of the EPA and will be one hour (+/-10%) in duration.
- You are required to bring and make available two hard copies of the Career Appraisal at the start of the interview.

- It will be held in a suitable space at your training provider.
- It is possible for your Professional Interview to be conducted remotely but please speak to your EPAO well in advance, as additional preparations will be required.

The questions asked by the panel will vary depending on their advance review of your Career Appraisal, but they are likely to centre on three principal lines of enquiry:

1. Explore the practical application of your knowledge and skills.
2. Validate your understanding of the behaviours.
3. Clarify the evidence in the Career Appraisal and verify that you were the author of it.

Expert perspective
by Paul Crosby

Paul Crosby, Head of Professional Practice Part 3 at the Architectural Association School of Architecture and experienced Part 3 Professional Examiner,[91] offers the following advice for preparing for the Professional Interview:

The Professional Interview is the culmination of at least five years in academia combined with professional practical experience before registering as an architect.

The interview is a professional conversation between the candidate and two assessors. The apprenticeship pathway typically consists of two interviews, several months apart and often conducted by the same assessors: the first focuses on the responses to the office-based scenario questions whereas the second considers the candidate's professional development.

Having experienced the first interview, the candidate is often reassured that it is not a grilling but a dialogue and an opportunity for them to expand on their experience in practice, showing professional judgment. In advance of the second interview, candidates have time to further reflect on their written responses and professional development and increase in confidence. All of which enables and encourages them to have a flowing discussion in which they convey their knowledge and, most importantly, offer proposals for better practice.

Experiential learning facilitates the chance for apprentices to instantly apply their learning in their work in practice. In so doing, they engage with colleagues, consultants and all stakeholders, thereby gaining a deeper understanding and appreciation of the collaborative effort required to realise a project.

Further, apprentices learn vicariously the important 'soft skills' not taught in school, such as communication and negotiation, bringing them to bear in the interview. In interview, I often witness apprentices showing a high level of professional maturity and offering nuanced responses balancing the theoretical with the reality of practice.

Paul has offered the following 'top tips' for a successful Professional Interview:

- Preparation. Read your written submissions in the period prior to the interview and reflect again on areas that you would further improve. In advance of the interview continue to engage in dialogue with colleagues in practice and your peer support group.
- In interview, aim to develop the topic, conveying your wider knowledge and understanding of the subject.
- When conveying knowledge, draw on your experience, giving examples of best practice.
- Knowing the 'answer' to every question is not essential. Understanding the process is important. Never guess.
- Allow your personality and character to come across.

EPA grading

Your performance in the EPA will determine the overall apprenticeship grade.[92] There are three potential outcomes: pass, merit or fail. Each individual assessment method will also be graded pass, merit or fail. To gain an apprenticeship pass or higher grade, you must achieve a minimum of a pass in each assessment component.

A pass grade represents full competence against the standard, whereas a merit grade suggests that an apprentice is demonstrating competence exceeding the standard. Factors such as the originality, insightfulness and criticality of evidence distinguish the two grades.

The following table shows the role of each assessment component grade in determining the overall grade:

Professional Interview supported by Career Appraisal	Case Study Report supported by Design Challenge	Overall Award
Merit	Merit	Merit
Merit	Pass	Pass
Pass	Merit	Pass
Pass	Pass	Pass
Fail	Pass	Fail
Pass	Fail	Fail
Fail	Fail	Fail

Table 3.3
Apprenticeship
grading matrix.

Apprentices who fail a component will be offered either a resit or retake. A retake involves a need for further learning before an assessment is taken, whereas a resit does not. In either case, it must take place within six months.

They may be required to undertake further work on the Career Appraisal and/or Case Study Report and may resubmit the same piece of work with changes. You will receive feedback outlining the area(s) failed in the EPA, but it will not outline what you need to do to overcome it in a resit or retake.

The maximum grade awarded to a resit or retake will be a pass unless the EPAO determines that extenuating circumstances accounted for the original fail.

Celebrating apprenticeship success

Architectural education, including the apprenticeship itself, is a long journey and it is therefore important to celebrate your achievements and successes along the way. This can be done in a variety of ways:

- Champion apprentices in the workplace.
- Celebrate achievement of certain milestones (e.g. graduation ceremonies).
- Enter eligible awards.

Degree shows

As you will remember from your undergraduate experiences, degree shows are an annual opportunity to showcase and celebrate the creative practice and achievements of all students, and this is no different for apprentices. In fact, you may have continued to attend them during your time in practice.

Unlike most full-time students, whether post-Part 1 or Part 2, you will be less preoccupied with getting hired and more interested in seeing the work of peers and professional networking. You may even be tasked by your practice to identify new talent.

**Figure 3.45
Northumbria University.** An exhibition of final-year degree apprenticeship projects as part of REVEAL: Architecture 2022.

Figure 3.46
Northumbria University, Harrison Lowthrop, Finding a Balance, Isle of Ulva. A socially focused masterplan enabling people to return to an under-threat remote Scottish community, rejuvenate it and secure a sustainable future (Part 2 Winner, RIBA North East Student Awards 2021).

Jane Redmond, Senior Associate at FaulknerBrowns Architects, says:

This four-year pathway through RIBA Part 2 and Part 3 encourages apprentices to design projects based on real-life situations, exploring practice challenges in imaginative ways[...] How refreshing it is to see students have such a clear understanding of how their architecture is composed, how it sits authentically and purposefully within the chosen context, harbouring so much of the identity of people and places that surround it.[93]

Student awards

Whilst the RIBA President's Medals Student Awards are considered the most prestigious and long-standing awards in architectural education in the world, there are an increasing number of student awards that reward talent, promote design innovation and encourage excellence in the study of architecture.

The following awards (not exhaustive) are open to apprentices, with nominees typically being selected by either their training provider or employer:

Category	Award	Training provider nominated	Employer nominated
RIBA International Student Awards	RIBA President's Medals (Silver)	•	
	RIBA President's Medals (Dissertation)	•	
RIBA Regional Student Awards	RIBA East	•	
	RIBA East Midlands	•	
	RIBA London	•	
	RIBA North East	•	
	RIBA North West	•	
	RIBA South and RIBA South East	•	
	RIBA South West and RIBA Wessex	•	
	RIBA West Midlands	•	
	RIBA Yorkshire	•	
Sponsored Awards	AJ Student Prize	•	
	3DReid Student Prize	•	
Thematic Student Awards	Architects for Health (AfH) Student Design Awards	•	
	SPAB Philip Webb Award	•	
	SAHGB Hawksmoor Essay Medal	•	
Sector Awards (e.g. Constructing Excellence Awards)	Technical Apprentice of the Year		•
	Higher Education Student of the Year		•
IfATE National Apprenticeship Awards	Apprentice of the Year		•
	Rising Star of the Year		•

Table 3.4 Some of the student awards open to Level 7 architecture apprentices.

Chapter 4
Professional life beyond the apprenticeship

Congratulations for completing your architecture apprenticeship and persevering through this route to registration. Given the many challenges associated with having to work and learn, and the demands of the course, you are now equipped with the knowledge, skills and behaviours that demonstrate the key competences needed in the profession and are part of a cohort of professionals sought after in the industry.

Although some of the terminology used may imply that your learning journey has ended, this is not the case, so you might ask yourself...

What's next?

Upon successfully completing your apprenticeship – after allowing yourself some time to relax and reflect – you might start to think, what next? By now, you may be working on projects with a good level of responsibility, but where do you go from here?

Ask any colleague and it is likely that they will respond with something about 'architecture being an ever-changing subject, with every day offering a new learning opportunity', and they will not be wrong. However, it is important for you to track your learning and professional ambitions to ensure that you meet your goals.

Learning does not stop at the end of your apprenticeship; instead, it should open opportunities to further develop your professional career. In this chapter, we have outlined a select number of specialist pathways you might pursue to

Figure 4.1 Bell Phillips Architects. Apprentices collaborating in a project design review in the office. A good way to listen to others and gain valuable professional experience.

help make early decisions about your career. Remember, these are not the only specialisms available to you but offer a flavour through a selection of certified and cognate fields. Knowledge of these specialisms might help plan your next three to five years in practice and determine how and where to develop your career.[1]

Professional registration

ARB registration
To register with the ARB, your training provider will need to ratify your grades at their assessment board and then upload your details to the ARB's 'pass list'. You need not do anything at this stage. The pass list enables the ARB to cross-reference application details to ensure that individuals have achieved the necessary qualifications to join the register. The same process will take place at the end of your Part 2 studies and at the end of your EPA.

Once uploaded, you can apply and your application will be reviewed by a committee who will email the outcome. It is a relatively simple process, but important items to note upon registration are:

- Your actions will be subject to the ARB Architects Code: Standards of Professional Conduct and Practice.[2]
  - Any issues that may arise from working with the public will be investigated by the Professional Conduct Committee.
- You are required to ensure that you have Professional Indemnity Insurance (PII) that covers you to a minimum level of £250,000.
  - PII ensures that the interests of you, your client and any users of your buildings are covered. The amount should reflect the scale and nature of the architectural work you carry out.
  - PII can cover individuals if you are working on projects alone, or your employer may have cover in place for you. It is **your** responsibility to ensure that the PII adequately covers the professional work you undertake.

RIBA Chartered Membership

Further to registration with the ARB, you can also apply for RIBA Chartered Membership.[3] Once you complete your apprenticeship, your student access will discontinue. To retain these benefits (and more), you will need to apply for Chartered Membership, which provides you access to the following:

- Connection with other chartered architects.
- Access to a range of CPD material and activities.
- Information and advice on topics related to, and in, the profession.
- Use of the RIBA crest and letters, and addition into the public directory.

ARB and RIBA mandatory CPD

With the introduction of the Building Safety Act 2022, the ARB has been given more powers to monitor the training of architects, particularly CPD activities.[4] The aim is to:

- ensure architects are committed to lifelong learning
- ensure architects maintain competence throughout their professional careers
- uphold public confidence in the profession.

The scheme is due to be launched in 2024 and will require architects to confirm that they have completed the CPD every year, compiled through a reflective statement on their development over the last 12 months. In principle, this intends to:

- improve overall competence (culture)
- be tailored to individual needs (relevance)
- be proportionate and deliverable (invest)
- avoid duplication, where possible (maximise opportunity).

Completion of the annual CPD will be a mandatory requirement of registration. There are currently no mandatory hours assigned, but a suggestion of eight events per year is likely.

The RIBA also obligates members to complete a minimum of 35 hours of CPD per year to maintain competence, which equates to approximately 45 minutes per week.[5] Twenty of these hours are required to be from the RIBA CPD core curriculum topics (two hours per topic). These activities also need to be recorded on the RIBA CPD recording manager.

RIBA advanced study and professional specialisms
The increasing complexities of the construction industry, coupled with the changing role and scope of the architect, suggest that the traditional route to the profession is no longer the only pathway available. Today, there are numerous specialisms that you can train for, so it is recommended that you plan your time and align your professional interests with employment. In such a dynamically changing profession, there is ample opportunity to carve out new roles aligned to a multitude of specialisms related to RIBA mandatory competences and CPD core curriculum.

Doctoral studies
Due to the length, cost and time involved in architectural education, many professionals were traditionally discouraged from continuing research. However, in recent years this attitude has changed with more architects and

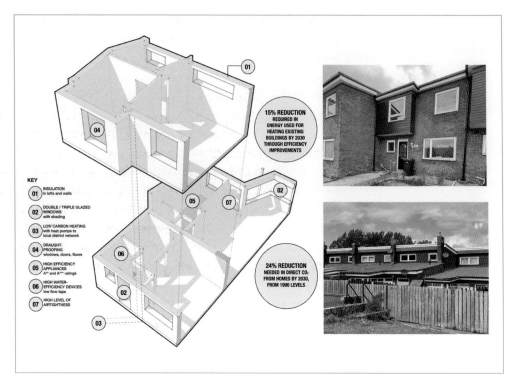

KEY

01 INSULATION
in lofts and walls

02 DOUBLE / TRIPLE GLAZED
WINDOWS
with shading

03 LOW CARBON HEATING
with heat pumps to
local district network

04 DRAUGHT-
PROOFING
windows, doors, floors

05 HIGH EFFICIENCY
APPLIANCES
A** and A*** ratings

06 HIGH WATER-
EFFICIENCY DEVICES
low flow taps

07 HIGH LEVEL OF
AIRTIGHTNESS

15% REDUCTION
REQUIRED IN
ENERGY USED FOR
HEATING EXISTING
BUILDINGS BY 2030
THROUGH EFFICIENCY
IMPROVEMENTS

24% REDUCTION
NEEDED IN DIRECT CO₂
FROM HOMES BY 2030,
FROM 1990 LEVELS

employers recognising the benefits of research to support innovation and increase productivity. This has been spurred by clients recognising the value of research and its impact on construction and the emphasis of government-led targets to monitor the industry. The nature of our profession allows for an extensive breadth of research topics – both practical and theoretical – and can add value to the wider construction industry particularly related to critical debates on sustainability, manufacturing, technology and safety. A PhD or doctorate is no longer only for those interested in academic pursuits but offers value in practice where certain employers now offer 'research time' and have research and development teams to support agile thinking and business diversification.[6]

Figure 4.2 Northumbria University, Dean Ireland, Social Housing Retrofits: Delivering Homes for the Future with YMCA Newcastle. This practice-based PhD involves the retrofit of existing, empty dwellings for young people to provide additional accommodation in the city and help alleviate the demand for social rented housing.

Academic researcher

Research in practice can be understood in a variety of ways, and research in architecture has become more widely recognised as the reciprocity between academia and industry strengthens. The opportunity for practice to utilise resources and expertise from universities is a key part of project success, driven by client aspirations, context, community engagement and building performance. The RIBA has determined three ways in which architects might engage with research:[7]

1. **Research knowledge:** how this knowledge can be integrated into a project.
2. **Research processes:** including techniques and finding knowledge, such as material tests, site reviews or obtaining archival information.
3. **Research resources:** ways of accessing knowledge, such as journals, archives or engaging with community and focus groups.

If you are interested in pursuing research, it is recommended you establish a plan to focus your aims and record your milestones. This will help develop your research interests and understand the resources needed to pursue them. A good place to improve awareness of current research themes and funding opportunities is through the government's UK Research and Innovation (UKRI) and the RIBA websites.[8, 9]

Principal Designer

The role of the Principal Designer (PD) is to plan, manage and monitor the pre-construction phase and to ensure that the construction work is carried out, as far as practically possible, without risk. This role is significant as it influences how a project is to be delivered to protect the health and safety of everyone affected. The publication of the *Building Safety Act 2022* sets out a framework from the government to deliver the principles and recommendations of Dame Judith Hackitt's report, 'Building a Safer Future, Independent Review of Building Regulations and Fire Safety: Final Report', and requires greater accountability and responsibility for safety issues throughout a building's lifecycle.[10] Architects play a significant role in its success.

The RIBA's Principal Designer course and register is a recognised accreditation for those managing the health and safety of projects, providing teams and clients with confidence through their competence. A PD needs to demonstrate health and safety skills, knowledge and experience to carry out the role. This means that you will need to have technical knowledge of the construction industry relevant to the project and understand, manage and coordinate the pre-construction phase, and design work in the construction phase. There are four key competences that a registered PD needs to demonstrate, these being:

1. Behavioural competence
2. Legislative and regulatory competence
3. Management competence
4. Technical frameworks competence.

For further detailed guidance on the competences required of a registered Principal Designer, you can refer to the RIBA Principal Designer competence criteria publication.[11] Below are some suggestions, if you are keen to explore this specialism:

- Find out if there is a PD in your practice and discuss the role and their experience.
- Ask to shadow a PD on a project and review documentation, recorded as part of your annual career appraisal.
- Review practice archive information associated with the role of the PD.
- If you do not have a PD in your practice, you could read documents pertaining to this role through the RIBA Bookshop or library.
- Discuss the benefits of this specialism with your employer and suggest participating in CPD activities as part of your career development.

Figure 4.3
FCBStudios.
Group study visit to
Woodlands Nursery
at Staffordshire
University, a net
zero timber
building, during
construction.

The role of the Principal Designer
by Richard Collis, Principal Designer, FCBStudios

The role of the Principal Designer (PD) is very significant as it proffers a legal responsibility to coordinate the health and safety of buildings in the pre-construction (design) stage. The PD is an integral part of the design team, managing the reduction of risks through collaboration. This requires technical and professional competence, and knowledge of how buildings are constructed, maintained and even demolished, as well as an understanding of new materials and methods of construction.

The role of the Principal Designer is aligned with, and often undertaken by, specialist architects. Health and safety used to be perceived as boring or bureaucratic, but the PD has a unique role in influencing the design process to help make buildings safer and healthier to construct and occupy. It provides opportunities for further specialist knowledge and provides a broader perspective of the influence of our designs within the realm of construction and wider society.

Client Advisor
The Client Advisor (CA) is an experienced architect who works with the client team but is not responsible for designing the building. Their role is to help the client manage the design process from its early stages and to assist in reviewing the quality, value, sustainability and life cycle of a building. This specialism requires several years' experience coupled with excellent communication and collaboration skills.

If you are keen to become a CA, you will need to demonstrate evidence across a range of sectors under four categories:

1. Knowledge
2. Skills and abilities
3. Understanding
4. Experience.

Your evidence must respond to six key activities:

1. Shaping vision and aspiration
2. Engaging stakeholders effectively
3. Supporting process to deliver outcomes
4. Facilitating value management
5. Preparing for use
6. In use.

You need to reflect on how you have added value to a project and discuss the types of clients and situations in which you have experience. It is good to reflect on the types of projects that you have been involved in, but also those you are keen to work on, along with your roles and responsibilities within a team. Since it might take some years to reach registration as a CA, we have offered a few suggestions to develop your experience:

- Understand the CA role related to the RIBA Plan of Work and consider its impact across all stages.
- Understand the CA Professional Services Contract and its scope of services.
- Participate in client meetings early on in projects to understand how briefs are developed, design teams constructed, risks managed and value added before design commences.
- Research the role through web pages such as the RIBA Client Advisor Toolkit.[12]
- Research whole-life strategies for buildings, sustainability targets and new technologies related to construction.

Client Advisors
by Helen Taylor, Director of Practice and RIBA Client Advisor, Scott Brownrigg

Client Advisors contribute their expertise and experience as designers. The role is very varied but might include providing independent technical advice for clients, helping a client choose the best team or ask the right questions. It might include research, evaluation or establishing design standards or guidance. It creates an opportunity to set a project off in the right direction and allow a client to engage the services of an architect, without committing to the whole project.

Figure 4.4 Scott Brownrigg, SHaW Academy. Sketch and visualisation for a multistorey secondary school on a restricted site, working closely with the client.

This role is for the apprentice who is keen to work directly with clients and have influence from an early stage. It is flexible and can be carried out independently, or as an additional role, with limited liability. Joining the RIBA Client Advisor Register demonstrates that a minimum, peer-reviewed standard has been met and can open doors to client relationships and an additional network.

Sustainability Consultant

More architects are choosing to specialise in areas of sustainability for ethical and professional reasons, and in order to offer greater services to clients, help define more environmentally conscious briefs and meet government sustainability targets. The scope of this specialism is broad, as it covers a variety of recognised accreditations and consultancy roles including:

- Passivhaus[13]
- BREEAM[14]
  - new construction
  - re-use
- One Click LCA[15]
- WELL certification[16]
- Living Building Challenge Certification[17]
- National Green Building Standard Green Verifier[18] (for residential buildings).

The range of accreditations helps maintain client confidence in the construction industry and ensures that architects are competent to lead, manage and deliver on sustainable targets. With so many different routes available, it may be difficult to know where to start, so it is recommended to discuss the benefits of specialist knowledge in sustainability with your employer and agree an appropriate way forward for the practice.

Figure 4.5 LEAP:
Lovingly Engineered
Architectural
Practice, Larch
Corner. A Passivhaus
project, using low-
carbon materials,
an air-source
heat pump and
photovoltaics array.

What is Passivhaus?
by Mark Siddall, Director of Architecture and Research, LEAP: Lovingly Engineered Architectural Practice

As an architect who takes the ethics of the profession seriously, when I learned that the buildings we are designing were not performing as they should, I became deeply troubled. They were uncomfortable, had poor air quality, used more energy, had higher bills and had higher carbon emissions than we – as a profession and an industry – were telling and selling to our clients. This frustrated my personal and professional ethics when I realised we were, in essence, selling faulty goods to clients and defrauding building owners and building users. With this awareness I committed to do something about it and eventually learned about the International Passivhaus Standard. Every time I challenged it, every time I questioned it, the evidence showed that it addressed many, if not all, the performance gaps. So, it was at this point I went on to become a Certified Passivhaus Designer/Consultant.

After the initial learning curve, I discovered that designing buildings to the Passivhaus Standard provided me with not only greater clarity and confidence, but also an excitement and inspiration that was lacking in other project work. I discovered new, meaningful design constraints that to this day help me make better buildings and encourage me to develop a new, contemporary architectural language that the future generations can love and enjoy. In my experience, if we are to design truly sustainable buildings, then the Passivhaus Standard is surely part of the answer.

Access Consultant

Inclusive design and accessibility in design can often be misunderstood, particularly for those outside architecture. The introduction of the Disability Discrimination Act 1995 (DDA), followed by the Equality Act 2010, created a significant opportunity for architects and other professionals to become registered Access Consultants through the National Register of Access Consultants.[19] The diverse nature of this role means that you might be advising in a technical capacity (building structure or construction), on procedures or policy, auditing existing environments, offering training for access and inclusive design, or assisting with funding applications. As we are more conscious of individual user requirements, the demand for Access Consultants has increased.

What is an Access Consultant?
by Fausto Pereira, Director, PH Partnership Architects

Access consultancy specialisation is significant for an architect because it focuses on ensuring that buildings and spaces are accessible and inclusive for all individuals, including those with impairments who are disabled by their environment. By understanding and implementing accessibility standards, architects can create environments that are usable and equitable, enhancing the quality of life for diverse populations. This specialisation informs future architectural practice by fostering a more inclusive design approach and promoting social responsibility. Architects trained in access consultancy will be equipped to address existing and future societal challenges related to accessibility, such as ageing populations and inclusive urban planning, creating more inclusive and sustainable built environments.

Access consultancy is an exciting field for me because it combines my passion for architecture with a strong desire to create inclusive spaces for all individuals. What attracted me to pursue this specialisation is the opportunity to make a meaningful impact on people's lives by ensuring that buildings and environments are accessible and barrier-free.

Apprentices should be committed to ensuring that they design with access in mind, and those considering this specialism are urged to join the closest regional group of the Access Association to network and to learn from experienced professionals. Concessionary membership for students is available. Additionally, working towards membership of the National Register of Access Consultants (NRAC) demonstrates credibility and expertise in the field.

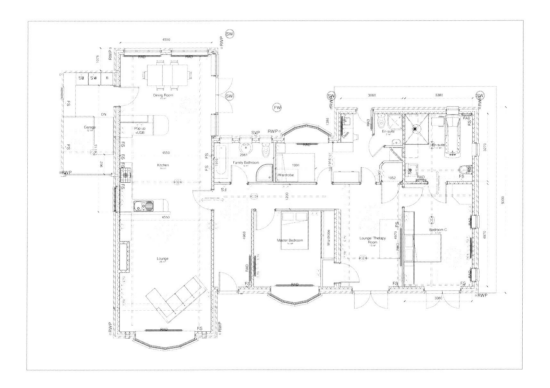

Figure 4.6
PH Partnership Architects. Examples of access design and its realisation. The influence of an Access Consultant can really alter the lives of people for the better.

Urban Designer

As the scale and complexity of projects increase, so do the demands for a team member with a strategic understanding of space and understanding of the impact and integration of design on existing environments, particularly as the scale of cities changes and the need for healthy public space grows. Urban Designers do not only work within urban contexts, they also research and analyse places to improve them. They may be involved in government policymaking, the development of design codes or take on the quality management role of buildings and places. It is a versatile role that can take you from the scale of one building to that of whole regions. Some of the key skills of an Urban Designer are:

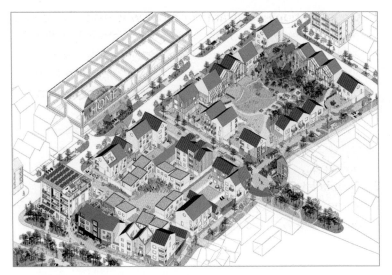

Figure 4.7 MawsonKerr Architects, Home of 2030. A competition-winning scheme examining multiple social, economic and cultural questions on communities and housing, as well as procurement concepts using scalable systems.

- understanding character and sense of place
- understanding human needs
- understanding how the built environment functions
- spatial awareness.[20]

Urban Designers do not typically work alone; an extensive part of the role is collaboration with teams of people and communication with different stakeholders, from clients to politicians and the public. The Urban Designer may be of interest to an individual keen to wear many hats and move between professional roles more fluidly.

Conservation Architect

The demand for Conservation Architects is another specialism on the rise in recent years, particularly as we build less and re-use more. Demolition should be the last option for a site, if the building can be safely managed and redesigned to reduce waste, pollution and laborious demolition processes. Managing and maintaining the longevity of our existing building stock is key if we seriously intend to reduce emissions and appreciate our environment. Today, the role has expanded far beyond the initial focus on building preservation to integrate new technologies and methodologies such as adaptive re-use, flexible design, 3D scanning and prototyping techniques. If you are interested in conservation, the RIBA currently offers three tiers of training and certification:

1. **Conservation Registrant:** for those who have awareness of the issues involved in working with historic buildings and have completed a course approved by the RIBA. This course is perfect if you are not currently working on historic or heritage buildings but are keen to learn about conservation.
2. **Conservation Architect:** for those with in-depth knowledge and experience of working with historic buildings.
3. **Specialist Conservation Architect:** for those with authoritative knowledge and practice experience of working with historic buildings.

Figure 4.8 HLM Architects, Matthew Morrish's sketch of a project with complex heritage restrictions. This early sketch helped to define the practice's approach to working with the existing building fabric.

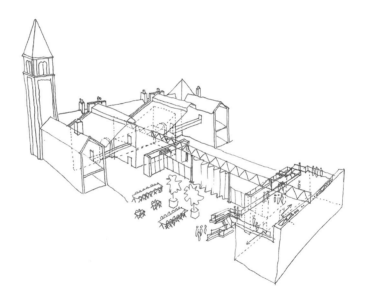

What is a Conversation Architect?
by Matthew Morrish, Conservation Architect, HLM Architects

Despite being a specialism within architecture, the breadth of the role of Conservation Architect is vast, from scheduled monuments dating back thousands of years to adapting and breathing new life into unloved twentieth-century industrial buildings. The scope is as varied as the history of the human habitat.

The philosophy and the practice of conservation and long-term sustainability are very similar in that they both believe in minimising the loss of existing built fabric and the loss of the embodied carbon that existing buildings constitute, thereby contributing to the fight against climate change.

Conservation can also address the intangible values that we assign to places and buildings, identifying the meaning they hold and to whom are they socially notable to conserve that significance.

Social and economic sustainability is often a consequence of the careful re-use of districts, streets, passages and buildings that are left-over or peripheral to mainstream economic activity, thereby allowing diverse economic and social activity to emerge and prosper. Being able to assert a recognised and accredited level of expertise, alongside the creativity that an architect can bring to their client's brief, can lead to fascinating architectural outcomes and a rewarding career.

BIM Manager

Building Information Modelling (BIM) is defined by the National Building Specification (NBS) as 'a process for creating and managing information on a construction project throughout its whole life cycle'.[21] The purpose of BIM is to allow for greater collaboration on design and information production for a project, particularly as team complexity and size increases. It may become a critical tool to document, monitor and manage our existing and future building stock, with the data contained in each model helping us learn more about building performance, user comfort and the impact of buildings on the environment. If you are interested in exploring this specialism, it is worth noting that this tool is not only for larger employers but offers lots of potential for small- and medium-sized practices to develop systems and obtain funding.

As BIM develops, so do extra resources to support its growth. Some of the key developments you might wish to explore are:

- Political reports that promote the benefits of BIM and consolidate its potential.

- Technology changes through clever product information specification, such as Building Element Modelling (BEM).
- Virtuality and how key construction resources will feed into BIM, such as building regulations, BREEAM and health and safety documents.
- Hardware developments, such as quantum computers and big data and the information that can be incorporated.
- Artificial intelligence integration with information, collaboration and teamwork.

What is BIM and its future in construction?
by Polina Pencheva, Associate, Morris+Company

Building Information Modelling (BIM) and digital technologies are rapidly changing the way we work as architects. Using big data and digital design will be key to achieve net zero targets and address future societal changes. Thus, having an expert understanding of BIM processes – how they promote collaboration and integration of data and how they impact design workflows, will give you a competitive advantage in the industry and can fast-track your career.

Many designers are concerned that embracing digital design and BIM can stifle creativity; however, I found the exact opposite to be true. Effective digital design processes can significantly reduce time spent on laborious, repetitive tasks and free more time for creativity. I was particularly drawn to BIM, as it makes collaboration and integration with all disciplines much more productive, allowing for cross-disciplinary learning and innovation in the process. I would advise apprentices to explore a variety of BIM software and test the limits in practice on a project they are working on. Don't be shy to be the BIM advocate.

There is currently no accredited BIM Manager course. However, the Royal Institute of Chartered Surveyors offers a Certificate in Building Information Modelling.[22] Moreover, the RIBA Bookshop has the publications *Understanding BIM* and *BIM Management Handbook*.[23, 24] So, if you are keen to become more advanced in using this tool, these resources are a good place to start.

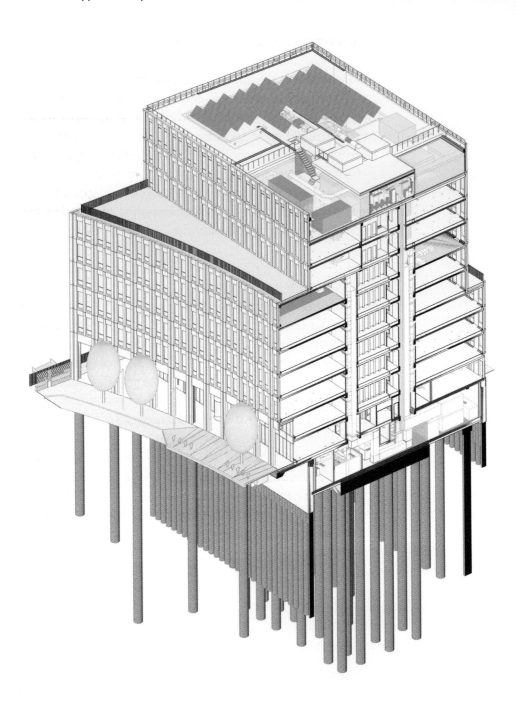

Figure 4.9
Morris+Company, an
in-progress BIM model.
BIM supports the live
sharing of information
between consultants
through a collaborative,
live model.

Supporting architecture apprenticeships

We hope that this handbook has proved to be a useful companion throughout your apprenticeship journey. Its purpose was to demystify the architecture apprenticeship route to qualification and share with you early lessons learned from apprentices, employers and training providers to help you make the most of it. Additionally, for those with an interest in advancing their career through a specialism, we hope it has provided you with essential information and encouragement to pursue it.

Despite your own apprenticeship journey concluding, there are many ways in which you can remain involved in architecture apprenticeships and support succession within the profession. Perhaps you could become an advocate for apprenticeships, mentor others on their journey, or you might want to continue practising and tutor apprentices at university. If you have gone on to specialise in climate science, research, ethics, conservation or net zero, be generous in sharing this knowledge and skills with others.

Finally, we hope that your journey has been a positive one and that you recognise the benefits of this route to make architecture a more diverse, inclusive and equitable profession, whilst fulfilling your role in improving the lives of others by upholding ethical practices.

Appendix A: Mapping of Assessment Methods

The table below maps the assessment methods against the knowledge, skills and behaviours required to meet the Architect Apprenticeship Standard. The content has been adapted from the EPA Plan.

	Knowledge An architect has an understanding of...
1. Design	**K1** • A range of advanced processes and techniques (e.g. digital fabrication) to generate, review and speculate on design proposals with multiple constraints, showing evidence of original thinking
2. History and Theory	**K2** • History of architecture and its impact on architectural practice • The cultural, social and intellectual histories, theories and technologies that influence the design of buildings
3. Fine Arts	**K3** • How the theories, practices and technologies of the arts influence architectural design and their creative application in design projects
4. Urban Design and Planning	**K4** • Urban design and town planning strategies and regulations • Process of obtaining planning permission (for example, drawings, reports, application)
5. People and Environment	**K5** • The in-depth relationships between users and buildings, between buildings and their environment, and the need to relate buildings and the spaces between them to diverse user needs and scale

Skills An architect is able to...	Professional Interview supported by Career Appraisal	Case Study Report supported by Design Challenge
S1 • Generate architectural design proposals • Evaluate and apply a comprehensive range of visual, oral and written media to test, analyse, critique and explain design proposals • Produce drawings and 3D models using relevant software, including Computer-Aided Design (CAD)	●	●
S2 • Apply understanding of current architectural debate to produce innovative solutions • Produce clear, logically argued and original written work relating to architectural culture, theory and design	●	
S3 • Apply fine art theories in a creative way that acknowledges their conceptualisation and representation	●	
S4 • Comply with relevant town planning policy throughout design and construction phases to obtain planning permission (for example, submitting planning application)		●
S5 • Identify end user needs, local and the social context in which the project is developed • Lead design development in respect of environmental context and sustainability		●

	Knowledge An architect has an understanding of...
6. Role of Architect	**K6** • The range of services offered by architects • The potential impact of building projects on existing and proposed communities and the related planning legislation • The context of the architect and the construction industry, including the architect's role in the processes of procurement and building production • The role of the architect within the design team and construction industry
7. Brief Analysis	**K7** • The client and design team briefing process, forms and terms of appointment • Methods of investigation and preparation of briefs for the design projects (for example, review of relevant precedent)
8. Structure, Construction and Engineering	**K8** • Structural, constructional and engineering considerations within building design, such as physical properties and characteristics of building materials, components and systems
9. Technologies	**K9** • Principles, systems and strategies for environmental comfort and building services, including sustainability principles • Alternative construction materials, processes and techniques that apply to design and construction, including the impact of materials on the environment • The role of Building Information Modelling (BIM), computational design and other relevant technologies used in the design process
10. Finance and Regulations	**K10** • Process of controlling building cost • Approved Documents for building regulations

Skills An architect is able to...	Professional Interview supported by Career Appraisal	Case Study Report supported by Design Challenge
S6 • Lead projects or parts of projects, taking into consideration business priorities and practice management • Deliver services in a responsible manner, prioritising the interests of the client and other stakeholders • Problem-solve and use professional judgment to take initiative and make appropriate decisions in situations with multiple constraints	●	
S7 • Critically review precedents relevant to the function, organisation and technological strategy of a design proposals • Prepare and develop a project brief (for example, by referring to RIBA Plan of Work)		●
S8 • Integrate knowledge of structural principles and construction techniques with building design	●	
S9 • Evaluate materials, processes and techniques that apply to architectural designs with multiple constraints and building construction, and how to integrate these into practicable design proposals • Apply various technological methods to building design to provide conditions of comfort and protection against the environment	●	
S10 • Meet client's brief within the constraints of the imposed budget limitations and building regulations		●

	Knowledge An architect has an understanding of...
11. Industry Context and Project Delivery	**K11** • Industries, organisations, regulations and procedures involved in translating design concepts into buildings and integrating plans into overall planning
12. Professionalism	**K12** • The nature of professionalism and the responsibilities of architects to clients, building users, constructors, professionals and the wider society
13. Clients, Users and Delivery of Services	**K13** • The obligations of architects to clients, stakeholders, warranties and third-parties • Client needs, appropriate communication methods, programming, coordination and competent delivery
14. Legal Framework and Processes	**K14** • The statutory legal context within which an architect must operate and what is required to ensure compliance with legal requirements or standards
15. Practice and Management	**K15** • Business priorities, required management processes and risks of running an architecture practice
16. Building Procurement	**K16** • UK construction and contract law, and construction procurement processes • The relationship between architects and other built environment professionals • Contractual relationships and the obligations of an architect acting as a contract administrator

Skills An architect is able to...	Professional Interview supported by Career Appraisal	Case Study Report supported by Design Challenge
S11 • Interact with statutory authorities (for example, planning or building control), private bodies (for example, developers) or individuals to competently deliver projects in a wide variety of sectors and within diverse legislative frameworks	●	
S12 • Act professionally when working independently and as part of a team, including communicating clearly with all stakeholders	●	
S13 • Offer impartial advice on construction-related issues, relevant legislation and risks • Identify and describe client and end user requirements, priorities and objectives		●
S14 • Work with an understanding of the relevant statutory and legal requirements during project development so that the risk of harm to those who build, use and maintain buildings is reduced	●	
S15 • Engage in business development and administration, including contributing to business strategy development, evaluating resources, planning, implementing and recording projects tasks • Supervise the work of junior staff including architectural assistants		●
S16 • Coordinate and engage in design team interaction • Resolve construction-related challenges and disputes, where appropriate • Undertake construction inspection responsibilities, including completing site visits and commenting on contractors' and sub-contractors' work in relation to architectural drawings	●	

Behaviours	An architect will exhibit the following behaviours:	Professional Interview supported by Career Appraisal	Case Study Report supported by Design Project/ Challenge
B1	Comply with the relevant professional codes of conduct (for example, ARB and RIBA)	●	
B2	Be honest and act with integrity, ethics and in a professional manner	●	
B3	Work singly, as part of a team or lead teams to provide a competent service		●
B4	Be organised and practise self-management when working independently		●
B5	Be conscious of the architect's obligation to the client, society and the profession	●	
B6	Be aware of individual level of competency and professional experience to ensure they are unlikely to bring the profession into disrepute		●
B7	Commit to identifying their own individual development needs and the obligation for Continuing Professional Development (CPD)	●	

Appendix B - List of higher education institutions offering the Architect (Level 7) Degree Apprenticeship

Higher Education Institution	RIBA Validated	ARB Prescribed	IfATE Training Provider
Birmingham City University	●	●	●
De Montfort University*	●	●	●
Leeds Beckett University	●	●	●
London Metropolitan University	●	●	●
London South Bank University	●	●	●
Northumbria University	●	●	●
Nottingham Trent University		●	●
Oxford Brookes University		●	●
Sheffield Hallam University	●	●	●
University of Bath*	●	●	●
University of Cambridge		●	●
University of Kent	●	●	●
University of Manchester / Manchester Metropolitan University		●	
University of Nottingham	●	●	●
University of Portsmouth	●	●	●
University of the West of England (UWE Bristol)	●	●	●

* Not currently recruiting apprentices.

References

Chapter 1

1. Doug Richard, 'The Richard Review of Apprenticeships', *Department for Business, Innovation & Skills*, https://www.gov.uk/government/publications/the-richard-review-of-apprenticeships, 2012 (accessed 9 September 2023).
2. Department for Education, 'How are apprenticeships funded and what is the apprenticeship levy?', *Blog: The Education Hub*, https://educationhub.blog.gov.uk/2023/03/10/how-are-apprenticeships-funded-and-what-is-the-apprenticeship-levy/, 2023 (accessed 9 September 2023).
3. Marion MacCormick, email to the authors, 11 January 2023.
4. *Ibid.*
5. Institute for Apprenticeship and Technical Education, 'Architect (Integrated Degree)', *Institute for Apprenticeship and Technical Education*, https://www.instituteforapprenticeships.org/apprenticeship-standards/architect-integrated-degree-v1-0, 2023 (accessed 9 September 2023).
6. A copy of the standard can be found in Appendix A. Please note that this standard is currently under review in response to proposed reforms to architectural education in the UK.
7. The End Point Assessment (EPA) Plan, including the Professional Interview supported by the Career Appraisal and Case Study Report supported by a Design Challenge, is comprehensively discussed and exemplified in Chapter 3.
8. The practice is now known as CREATE SOUTH WEST following acquisition by CREATE and Jason Jarvis.
9. The survey was conducted by the authors for the exclusive purpose of this handbook and the findings presented at the Innovation in Built Environment Education (iBEE) Conference at Liverpool John Moores University on 4–5 April 2023. The survey returned 59 responses from apprentices at eight different training providers.
10. Will Hurst, 'Why would anyone choose to study architecture?', *Architects' Journal*, https://www.architectsjournal.co.uk/news/opinion/why-would-anyone-choose-to-study-architecture, 2017 (accessed 24 December 2022).
11. HomeGrown Plus is a not-for-profit organisation dedicated to improving diversity within architecture and the creative industries. Further information can be found at homegrownplus.co.uk
12. As well as founding HomeGrown Plus, Neil is a trustee of BluePrint for All (formerly the Stephen Lawrence Charitable Trust), Honorary Professor at The Bartlett School of Architecture, RIBA Honorary Fellow and recipient of the 2022 AJ 100 Contribution to the Profession award.
13. The collective term 'Global Majority' was coined by Rosemary Campbell-Stephens as an alternative to racialised terms such as 'Black, Asian and Minority Ethnic' (BAME).
14. Archilogues was initiated by Faith Muir, Level 7 Architecture Apprentice at Foster + Partners and the University of Bath. It is available online via LinkedIn: https://www.linkedin.com/company/archilogues/ and Instagram: @archi.logues
15. Royal Institute for British Architects / Mirza & Nacey Research, *RIBA Education Statistics 2020/21*, RIBA Education Department, London, UK, 2022, p 21.
16. For further reading see: Peter Holgate, 'Developing an inclusive curriculum of architecture for students with dyslexia', *Art, Design and Communication in Higher Education*, Vol. 14, issue 1, 2015, pp 87-99.
17. Kaye (1960) explains that a pupil would pay 'a premium to the architect at the commencement of [...] his training, whereas the apprentice [paid] for his training in kind by his services. [...] Gentlemen's sons entering the profession would become pupils, while such members of the artisan class as aspired to be architects might enter an apprenticeship of five or six years.' Barrington Kaye, *The Development of the Architectural Profession in Britain: A Sociological Study*, Allen & Unwin, London, 1960, p 48.
18. The Institute of British Architects was founded in 1834, gaining its Royal Charter in 1837. The Architects (Registration) Acts of 1931-1938 restricted the legal use of the title Architect to those who had passed the RIBA's Intermediate and Final Examinations – voluntary when first introduced in 1864, compulsory for RIBA Associateship from 1882.
19. Lionel Budden, 'A Proposal for the Development of Architectural Education in the United Kingdom', *The Architectural Review*, December 1912, pp 317-23 (322).
20. Leslie Martin, 'Report on the Conference of Architectural Education', *RIBA Journal*, June 1958, pp 279-82.
21. Richard Gardner, 'The Development of Architectural Education in the UK', *Architects' Journal*, 9 October 1974, pp 873-81 (880).
22. Established as a statutory body by Parliament through the Architects Act 1997.
23. Please note that not all UK architecture qualifications are prescribed by the ARB. A list of architecture qualifications, including degree apprenticeships, prescribed by the ARB for the purposes of admission to the UK Register of Architects can be found at https://arb.org.uk/student-information/schools-institutions-architecture/
24. You can check whether an architecture course is RIBA validated at https://www.architecture.com/education-cpd-and-careers/riba-validation/riba-validated-schools-uk
25. The RIBA Themes and Values for Architectural Education (T+V4AE) are discussed in Chapter 3, 'How do I make the most of my apprenticeship?'
26. Accessible at: https://reports.ofsted.gov.uk/.
27. Adapted from: Peter Holgate, *Presentation to Degree Apprentices in Architecture*, 2022, Northumbria University, Newcastle upon Tyne, UK.
28. The ISA is further discussed in Chapter 2 and may result in exemption from select modules based on prior learning (or equivalent).
29. The Office of Qualifications and Examinations Regulator (Ofqual) acts as the EQA provider for the majority of apprenticeship standards.
30. Adapted and updated from: Neil Spiller, *How to Thrive at Architecture School: A Student Guide*, RIBA Publishing, London, 2020, p 14, and Jenny Russell and Andrew Thompson, *Study Architecture Well*, Royal Institute of British Architects, London, 2021, p 16.
31. Calculated on new entrants to Part 2 from 2016/17 to 2020/21 contained in: Royal Institute for British Architects / Mirza & Nacey Research, *RIBA Education Statistics 2020/21*, RIBA Education Department, London, 2022, p 10.
32. *Ibid.*
33. To be eligible, you must complete the course within four academic years (no more than twice the length of the equivalent full-time course). Those studying for an ARB accredited Master of Architecture (MArch) qualification full-time, are asked to apply for undergraduate funding support, but this does not apply to those studying part-time.
34. Will Hunter, 'Alternative Routes for Architecture?', *The Architectural Review*, https://www.architectural-review.com/today/alternative-routes-for-architecture, 2012 (accessed 23 December 2022).
35. The LSA has an academic partnership with the University of Liverpool as a prerequisite for home students' eligibility for student finance for tuition fee and maintenance loans through the Student Loans Company.
36. Students may achieve a saving on tuition fees through a salary sacrifice arrangement with their practice. It is important to ensure that your earnings (after salary sacrifice) remain above the National Minimum Wage threshold.
37. According to the RIBA Diploma Guide, Syllabus and Regulations 2022-23 (p 21), full-time employment is deemed to be met by working at least 1,250 hours per annum or 24 hours per week.
38. Personal tutors must possess a minimum of three years' experience as both a registered architect in the country where you are working and design tutor in architectural education, and be independent of your practice. Tutors must also have a substantial role teaching architectural design in a School of Architecture and must be approved by the programme director.
39. Kirk McCormack, 'How do we learn to be architects?', *The RIBA Journal*, https://www.ribaj.com/intelligence/how-do-we-learn-to-be-architects, 2015 (accessed 22 December 2022).
40. The survey was conducted by the authors for the exclusive purpose of this handbook and the findings presented at the Innovation in Built Environment Education (iBEE) Conference at Liverpool John Moores University on 4–5 April 2023. The survey returned 59 responses from apprentices at eight different training providers.
41. Note that opportunities for reciprocity between workplace and academic learning vary significantly. We recommend speaking with prospective training providers about the extent to which workplace learning might be accommodated within the curriculum.
42. Challenges incidental to the coronavirus (COVID-19) pandemic were excluded, as they were believed to be of little to no long-term impact to student experience.
43. Marion MacCormick, email to the authors, 11 January 2023.

Chapter 2

1. UK Government, *National Minimum Wage and National Living Wage rates*, https://www.gov.uk/national-minimum-wage-rates (accessed 4 January 2023).
2. Ofsted, *Ofsted Strategy 2022-2027, Our guiding principle*, https://assets.publishing.service.gov.uk/media/626677e3e90e07168ced91b2/Ofsted_Strategy_2022_2027_summary.pdf (accessed 4 January 2023).
3. Royal Institute of British Architects, *RIBA Plan of Work 2020, Architecture*, https://www.architecture.com/knowledge-and-resources/resources-landing-page/riba-plan-of-work, 2020 (accessed 15 November 2022).
4. Royal Institute of British Architects, *RIBA Code of Conduct 2019*, https://www.architecture.com/knowledge-and-resources/resources-landing-page/code-of-professional-conduct, 2019 (accessed 15 November 2022).
5. Royal Institute of British Architects, *Equality, diversity and inclusion*, https://www.architecture.com/about/equality-diversity-and-inclusion (accessed 18 November 2022).
6. There are a huge number of resources and groups taking positive

action in the built environment. Some of these groups include Architecture for Change.org, Architectureforall.org, Blackfemarc. com, Paradigm Network, Built by Us, Architects Climate Action Network, and Architects Declare. If you are interested in getting involved, you should make contact.

7.   Royal Institute of British Architects, *RIBA Jobs*, https://jobs. architecture.com/ (accessed 18 November 2022).

8.   Royal Institute of British Architects, *Tips for CVs aimed at Part 1 roles*, https://jobs.architecture.com/article/writing-your-first-cv-for-part-1-year-out-architecture-jobs/ (accessed 18 November 2022).

9.   Living Wage Foundation, *For the real cost of living*, https://www. livingwage.org.uk/ (accessed 2 September 2023).

10. UVW-SAW, 'An architectural assistant's guide to employment rights', *Architects' Journal*, https://www.architectsjournal.co.uk/news/an-architectural-assistants-guide-to-employment-rights, 24 March 2021 (accessed 5 January 2023).

11. Section of Architectural Workers SAW, 'End unpaid overtime', *Section of Architectural Workers*, https://uvw-saw.org.uk/ (accessed 5 January 2023).

12. Royal Institute of British Architects, *What does our Business Benchmarking Report tell us about architects' salaries*, https://jobs. architecture.com/staticpages/10290/what-does-our-business-benchmarking-report-tell-us-about-architects-salaries/ (accessed 5 January 2023).

13. Some apprentices have also been using the title *Senior Architectural Assistant*, which is also permissible.

14. Living Wage Foundation, What is it?, *Living Wage Foundation*, https://www.livingwage.org.uk/what-real-living-wage#:~:text=The%20London%20Living%20Wage%20is,currently%20%C2%A310.90%20per%20hour (accessed 2 September 2023).

15. Based on 59 responses from apprentices at eight different training providers to a survey conducted by the authors for the exclusive purpose of this handbook. The findings were presented at the Innovation in Built Environment Education (iBEE) Conference at Liverpool John Moores University on 4-5 April 2023.

16. UK Government, 'Finding an end-point assessment organisation', *UK Government*, https://www.gov.uk/government/publications/finding-an-end-point-assessment-organisation (accessed 18 January 2023).

17. UK Government, 'Conditions for being on the register of end-point assessment organisations', https://www.gov.uk/guidance/conditions-for-being-on-the-register-of-end-point-assessment-organisations (accessed 20 November 2023).

18. UK Government, 'Become an apprentice', *UK Government*, https:// www.gov.uk/become-apprentice (accessed 18 January 2023).

19. If you are currently enrolled on a full-time or part-time course in architecture at postgraduate level and wish to transfer to an apprenticeship, you must discuss this with your training provider. Each will have their respective procedures that must be followed; they will also determine whether it is possible, depending on the stage you are at on your postgraduate course.

20. NI Direct, 'Apprenticeships, if you're ready, they're waiting', *NI Direct government services*, https://www.nidirect.gov.uk/campaigns/apprenticeships (accessed 18 January 2023).

21. Apprenticeships.scot, 'Kick-start your career with an apprenticeship', *apprenticeships.scot*, https://www.apprenticeships. scot/ (accessed 18 January 2023).

22. Welsh Government, 'Make a genius decision with apprenticeships', *Welsh Government*, https://www.gov.wales/apprenticeships-genius-decision (accessed 18 January 2023).

23. UK Government, 'Apprenticeships: initial assessment to recognise prior learning', *UK Government*, https://www.gov.uk/government/publications/apprenticeships-recognition-of-prior-learning/apprenticeships-initial-assessment-to-recognise-prior-learning (accessed 8 February 2023).

24. UK Government, 'Apprenticeships: off-the-job training', *UK Government*, https://www.gov.uk/government/publications/apprenticeships-off-the-job-training (accessed 8 February 2023).

25. J. Russell, M. Thompson and A. Jones, 'Study Architecture Well', *RIBA Architecture*, pp 22-50, https://pureadmin.qub.ac.uk/ws/portalfiles/portal/400109780/RIBA_Study_Architecture_Wellpdf_4. pdf, 2021 (accessed 12 February 2023).

Chapter 3

1.   Malcolm Knowles, *Andragogy in Action: Applying Modern Principles of Adult Education*, Jossey Bass, San Francisco, CA, 1984.

2.   Learning and Work Institute, 'Line Manager Guide to Apprenticeship', *Learning and Work Institute*, https://learningand work.org.uk/wp-content/uploads/2021/10/Line-manager-guide-to-apprenticeships.pdf, undated (accessed 31 July 2023).

3.   RIBA, 'RIBA PEDR: Your professional development record', *RIBA*, https://www.architecture.com/education-cpd-and-careers/studying-architecture/riba-pedr, 2023 (accessed 29 July 2023).

4.   While other job titles may be used to describe this role, including Skills Coach and Apprenticeship Skills Reviewer, the overall role and responsibilities are essentially the same.

5.   Prevent is part of CONTEST, the government's counter-terrorism strategy, and is intended to counter terrorist ideology and challenge those who promote it, doing so by working with sectors and institutions where the risk of radicalisation is assessed to be high.

6.   YAPF, led by a committee of local RIBA members and supported by the RIBA, promotes and supports young architectural practitioners (up to eight years post-qualification) in the North East region to build networks across the profession and cognate professions.

7.   RIBA, 'The Way Ahead: An introduction to the new RIBA Education and Professional Framework and an overview of its key components', *RIBA*, https://riba-prd-assets.azureedge.net/-/media/GatherContent/Business-Benchmarking/Additional-Documents/RIBA-The-Way-Ahead-brochurepdf.pdf, 2020 (accessed 19 May 2023).

8.   Delivered in partnership with the RIBA and carried no credit weighting.

9.   RIBA, 'RIBA Procedures for Validation [for UK and international course in architecture]', *RIBA*, https://riba-prd-assets.azureedge. net/-/media/Files/2021-RIBA-validation-procedures.pdf, 2021, p 11 (accessed 19 May 2023).

10. RIBA, 'Procedures for Validation', p 80.

11. Dieter Bentley-Gockmann, *RIBA Health and Safety Guide*, RIBA Publishing, London, 2023.

12. Matt Milton, 'Learn about the relaunched RIBA Health and Safety Test', *RIBA*, https://www.architecture.com/knowledge-and-resources/knowledge-landing-page/learn-about-the-relaunched-riba-health-and-safety-test, 2021 (accessed 30 July 2023).

13. HSE, 'Construction statistics in Great Britain, 2022', *HSE*, https://www.hse.gov.uk/statistics/assets/docs/ridind.xlsx, 2022 (accessed 29 July 2023).

14. The Principal Designer is a role that you can specialise into as you become a more experienced practitioner. We discuss this role in more detail in Chapter 4 (p213).

15. Architect's Mental Wellbeing Forum, 'Architect's Mental Wellbeing Toolkit', *Mental Health at Work*, https://docs.wixstatic.com/ugd/fb91f8_33c556b0fe9b4855824da571826586d6.pdf; HSE, 'Construction statistics in Great Britain, 2022', *HSE, https://www.hse.gov.uk/statistics/industry/construction.pdf*, 2022 (accessed 29 July 2023).

16. RIBA, 'Procedures for Validation', p 80.

17. RIBA, 'RIBA Code of Professional Conduct', *RIBA, https://www. architecture.com/knowledge-and-resources/resources-landing-page/code-of-professional-conduct*, 2023 (accessed 12 July 2023).

18. RIBA, 'RIBA Code of Practice for Chartered Practices', *RIBA,* https://www.architecture.com/knowledge-and-resources/resources-landing-page/code-of-practice-for-chartered-practices, 2021 (accessed 12 July 2023).

19. ARB, 'The Architects Code: Standards of Professional Conduct and Practice', *ARB*, https://arb.org.uk/wp-content/uploads/2016/05/Architects-Code-2017.pdf, 2017 (accessed 12 July 2023).

20. See: https://www.architectsdeclare.com/ (accessed 31 July 2023).

21. RIBA, 'RIBA Ethical Practice Knowledge Schedule', *RIBA*, https://riba-prd-assets.azureedge.net/-/media/GatherContent/Mandatory-competences/Additional-documents/RIBA-Knowledge-Schedule-Ethical-Practice-March-2021.pdf, 2021 (accessed 4 July 2023).

22. Carys Rowlands and Alasdair Ben Dixon, *RIBA Ethical Practice Guide*, RIBA Publishing, London, 2023, pp 10-13.

23. Alasdair Ben Dixon, 'How to spot an ethical dilemma - and what to do about it', *The RIBA Journal*, https://www.ribaj.com/intelligence/ethical-practice-guide-book-alasdair-ben-dixon-collective-works, 2023 (accessed 24 September 2023).

24. RIBA, 'Procedures for Validation', p 80.

25. RIBA, '2030 Climate Challenge', *RIBA*, https://www.architecture. com/about/policy/climate-action/2030-climate-challenge, 2023 (accessed 30 July 2023).

26. RIBA, 'Sustainable Outcomes Guide', *RIBA*, https://www. architecture.com/knowledge-and-resources/resources-landing-page/sustainable-outcomes-guide, 2019 (accessed 30 July 2023).

27. RIBA, 'Procedures for Validation', p 10.

28. Architects Declare, 'Practice Guide 2021', *Architects Declare*, https://www.architectsdeclare.com/uploads/AD-Practice-Guide-2021-v1_3.pdf, 2021 (accessed 1 August 2023).

29. Delivered as part of the Architect (Level 7) apprenticeship at University of Cambridge.

30. Delivered as part of the Architect (Level 7) apprenticeship at London South Bank University.

31. Available at: https://www.architectscan.org/ (accessed 31 July 2023).

32. Available at: https://www.architectsdeclare.com/uploads/AD-Practice-Guide-2021-v1_3.pdf (accessed 31 July 2023).

33. Available at: https://www.leti.uk/ (accessed 31 July 2023).

34. Available at: https://riba-academy.architecture.com/ (accessed 31 July 2023).

35. Available at: https://www.climateframework.com/library-intro (accessed 31 July 2023).

36. Available at: https://www.supplychainschool.co.uk/topics/sustainability/ (accessed 31 July 2023).

37. Sofia Pelsmaker, Aidan Hoggard, Urszula Kozminska and Elizabeth Donovan, *Designing for the Climate Emergency: A Guide for Architecture Students*, RIBA Publishing, London, 2022.
38. This is an alternative to a traditional Master's dissertation and affords learners an opportunity to demonstrate and apply scholarship and inquiry to a self-selected area of interest in architecture or related, wider cultural context. The investigation may employ creative practice, visual and architectural methods, and result in artefactual outputs as forms of research, in addition to written.
39. Zaid Alwan possesses academic and commercial expertise in low-carbon design and sustainable construction. Zaid is a BREEAM and Low Carbon Assessor, has published on whole energy systems and their integration into BIM platforms and, as a member of the BIM Academic Forum, champions BIM approaches to higher education curricula.
40. For more information on the project, please see: https://norr.com/project/stephenson-building-engineering-hub/
41. RIBA, 2030 Climate Challenge.
42. Whole-life carbon review tools include FCBS CARBON (https://portal.fcbstudios.com/fcbscarbon) and H\B:ERT (https://www.hawkinsbrown.com/sub-services/hbert-emissions-reduction-tool/) (accessed 31 July 2023).
43. RIBA, 'Procedures for Validation', p 80.
44. In lieu of a dissertation, some training providers have opted for either a research paper or extended essay. Whilst the requirements of these assessment methods vary, the following guidance is just as applicable, and the resultant learning against the KSBs of the apprenticeship standard is similar.
45. Christopher Frayling, 'Research in art and design', *Royal College of Art: Research Papers*, Vol. 1, number 1, 1993.
46. Nigel Cross, 'Designerly ways of knowing', *Design Studies*, Vol. 3, issue 4, 1982, pp 221-27.
47. *BUM* is a Helsinki-based, risograph printed arts, architecture and culture publication produced in 150-only hand-numbered editions. *BUM Edition 6: Order* contains contributions by international artists, writers, architects and designers.
48. Further information can be found at: https://fcbstudios.com/practice/explore/daniel-zepeda-rivas (accessed 31 July 2023).
49. Further information can be found at: https://www.ryderarchitecture.com/wp-content/uploads/2023/06/Closing-the-Loop-1.pdf (accessed 31 July 2023).
50. Available at: https://server.fcbstudios.com/files/download?name=Anti-ableist-Design-Guide.pdf (accessed 31 July 2023).
51. RIBA, 'Inclusive Design Overlay to the RIBA Plan of Work', *RIBA*, https://www.architecture.com/knowledge-and-resources/resources-landing-page/inclusive-design-overlay-to-riba-plan-of-work, 2023 (accessed 30 July 2023).
52. The Housing Quality Indicator (HQI) system is a measurement and assessment tool to evaluate housing schemes based on quality rather than simply cost. It can be accessed at: https://www.gov.uk/guidance/housing-quality-indicators (accessed 31 July 2023).
53. Design for Homes is a not-for-profit research foundation that champions the value of good design in the housing industry. It can be accessed at: https://www.designforhomes.org/ (accessed 31 July 2023).
54. The project won the SLA Student Award 2020 and was showcased at the (Venice) Biennale Architettura 2021.
55. Rob Fiehn, Kyle Buchanan and Mellis Haward, *Collective Action!: The Power of Collaboration and Co-Design in Architecture*, RIBA Publishing, London, 2023.
56. RIBA, 'Procedures for Validation', p 81.
57. *Ibid*, p 10.
58. Rosie Parnell and Rachel Sara, *The Crit: An Architecture Student's Handbook*, Routledge, London, 2006.
59. Available at: http://www.presidentsmedals.com (accessed 31 July 2023).
60. Available at: https://www.architectsforhealth.com/awards/ (accessed 31 July 2023).
61. Available at: https://architectureprize.com/
62. Available at: https://www.architectsjournal.co.uk/practice/students/aj-student-prize
63. RIBA, 'Procedures for Validation', p 81.
64. Available at: https://employeeownership.co.uk/ (accessed 31 July 2023).
65. Mark Kemp, *Good Practice Guide: Business Resilience*, RIBA Publishing, London, 2022.
66. RIBA, 'RIBA Business Resilience Roadmap', *RIBA*, https://www.architecture.com/knowledge-and-resources/resources-landing-page/Business-Resilience-Roadmap, 2023 (accessed 30 July 2023).
67. RIBA, '12 Golden Rules: The importance of having a written form of appointment', *RIBA Contracts*, https://riba-prd-assets.azureedge.net/-/media/Files/Contracts/RIBA-12-Golden-Rules-A4-for-PDF-final-version_V2.pdf, 2023 (accessed 30 July 2023).
68. Jan Knikker, *How To Win Work: The architect's guide to business development and marketing*, RIBA Publishing, London, 2021.
69. Simon Foxell, *Starting a Practice: A Plan of Work*, RIBA Publishing, 3rd edition, London, 2021.
70. Nigel Ostime, *Handbook of Practice Management*, RIBA Publishing, 10th edition, 2024.
71. RIBA, 'RIBA Benchmarking: 2023 Changes', *RIBA*, https://www.architecture.com/knowledge-and-resources/resources-landing-page/riba-benchmarking-2023-changes, 2023 (accessed 30 July 2023).
72. SKA rating, developed by the Royal Institution of Chartered Surveyors, aims to encourage good practice in fit-out projects to help assess and benchmark the sustainability of them, covering more than 100 'good practice' measures.
73. Available at: https://www.iod.com/ (accessed 31 July 2023).
74. Available at: https://www.fsb.org.uk (accessed 31 July 2023).
75. Available at: https://www.britishchambers.org.uk/ (accessed 31 July 2023).
76. Mark Kemp, *Good Practice Guide*.
77. Richard Brindley, *Good Practice Guide: Professionalism at Work*, RIBA Publishing, London, 2022.
78. Stephen Brookhouse and Peter Farrall, *Good Practice Guide: Fees*, RIBA Publishing, London, 2021.
79. RIBA, 'Procedures for Validation', p 11.
80. Stephen is also a member of Architecture Apprenticeships Trailblazer Group, End Point Assessor and Part 3 Professional Examiner, major contributor to Northumbria University's Architect (Level 7) Degree Apprenticeship in Architecture and former Part 3 course leader at the University of Westminster.
81. Stephen Brookhouse, *Part 3 Handbook*, RIBA Publishing, London, 2020.
82. Institute for Apprenticeships and Technical Education, 'End Point Assessment Plan for Architect Apprenticeship (Level 7)', *Institute for Apprenticeships and Technical Education*, https://www.instituteforapprenticeships.org/media/1cwj5ocx/st0533_architect_l7_epa_v11_nov23.pdf, 2023, p 7-8 (accessed 7 December 2023).
83. *Ibid*.
84. *Ibid*.
85. *Ibid*.
86. *Ibid*.
87. For further information on the external quality assurance of apprenticeships, see: https://www.instituteforapprenticeships.org/quality/external-quality-assurance/ (accessed 10 September 2023).
88. Institute for Apprenticeships and Technical Education, 'End Point Assessment Plan for Architect Apprenticeship (Level 7)', p 6.
89. *Ibid*.
90. *Ibid*, p 7.
91. Paul has served as a professional examiner at Cardiff University, Northumbria University, University of Bath, University of Westminster and the RIBA and is an external examiner at Oxford Brookes University. He is also co-author of the book, *Architect: The Evolving Story of a Profession*, RIBA Publishing, London, 2023.
92. Institute for Apprenticeships and Technical Education, 'End Point Assessment Plan for Architect Apprenticeship (Level 7)', *Institute for Apprenticeships and Technical Education*, https://www.instituteforapprenticeships.org/media/1924/st0533_architect_l7_ap-for-publication_22062018.pdf, 2018, p 10 (accessed 4 July 2023).
93. Jane Redmond, '"Quality over quantity": Northumbria Student Show 2022', *Architects' Journal*, https://www.architectsjournal.co.uk/practice/students/quality-over-quantity-northumbria-student-show-2022, 2022 (accessed 4 July 2023).

Chapter 4

1. Certain practices might be better suited to certain specialisms than others, due to type and scale of projects that they design, or office size and location. This chapter aims to help you understand more about each specialism as part of your Continuing Professional Development and hear from specialists in each area.
2. Architects Registration Board (ARB), 'The Architects Code: Standards of Professional Conduct and Practice', *ARB*, London, Architects Registration Board, 2017, https://arb.org.uk/wp-content/uploads/2016/05/Architects-Code-2017.pdf (accessed 28 June 2023).
3. Royal Institute of British Architects (RIBA), *Join the RIBA: Individual Chartered Membership*, https://www.architecture.com/join-riba/individual-chartered-membership (accessed 28 June 2023).
4. Architects Registration Board (ARB), *Scheme for Continuing Professional Development*, https://arb.org.uk/architect-information/maintaining-registration/maintaining-competence/scheme-for-continuing-professional-development-cpd/ (accessed 28 June 2023).
5. Royal Institute of British Architects (RIBA) CPD, *What are the CPD obligations for RIBA Chartered Architects?*, https://www.ribacpd.com/information/cpdobligationsforribacharteredarchitects.aspx#:~:text=RIBA%20CPD%20programme%3F-,What%20are%20the%20CPD%20obligations%20for%20RIBA%20Chartered%20Architects%3F,of%20CPD%20to%20maintain%20competence (accessed 29 June 2023).
6. A PhD is typically an academic degree, while a doctorate can be either academic or professional.
7. Royal Institute of British Architects (RIBA), *How architects use research*, https://www.architecture.com/knowledge-and-

resources/resources-landing-page/how-architects-use-research (accessed 29 June 2023).

8. UK Research and Innovation (UKRI), *Innovate UK*, https://www.ukri.org/councils/innovate-uk/ (accessed 29 June 2023).

9. Royal Institute of British Architects (RIBA), *Supporting research projects*, https://www.architecture.com/knowledge-and-resources/resources-landing-page/supporting-research-projects (accessed 29 June 2023).

10. Dame J. Hackitt, 'Building a Safer Future, Independent Review of Building Regulations and Fire Safety: Final Report', *Gov.UK*, UK, APS Group, 2018, https://assets.publishing.service.gov.uk/government/uploads/system/uploads/attachment_data/file/707785/Building_a_Safer_Future_-_web.pdf (accessed 2 July 2023).

11. Royal Institute of British Architects (RIBA), *RIBA Principal Designer register competence criteria*, https://www.architecture.com/knowledge-and-resources/resources-landing-page/riba-principal-designer-register-competence-criteria#available-resources (accessed 5 June 2023).

12. Royal Institute of British Architects (RIBA), *Client Advisor Toolkit*, https://www.architecture.com/knowledge-and-resources/resources-landing-page/client-adviser-toolkit (accessed 5 June 2023).

13. Passivhaus Trust, *The UK Passive House Organisation*, https://www.passivhaustrust.org.uk/ (accessed 8 June 2023).

14. Building Research Establishment (BRE), *BREEAM*, https://bregroup.com/products/breeam/#:~:text=BREEAM%20is%20the%20world's%20leading,construction%2C%20to%20use%20and%20refurbishment (accessed 8 June 2023).

15. One Click LCA, *Calculate your environmental impact in minutes*, www.oneclicklca.com (accessed 8 June 2023).

16. International Well Building Institute, *Introduction to Well*, https://well.support/introduction-to-well-682f7166-0d14-45fa-8d5b-ffca9e4c0b59 (accessed 8 June 2023).

17. International Living Future Institute, *About*, https://living-future.org/about/ (accessed 8 June 2023).

18. National Green Building Standard (NGBS), Home Innovation Research Labs, *The NGBS green promise*, https://www.ngbs.com/the-ngbs-green-promise (accessed 8 June 2023).

19. National Register of Access Consultants, *Welcome*, https://www.nrac.org.uk/ (accessed 25 November 2023).

20. R. Cowan, *Essential Urban Design: A Handbook for Architects, Designers and Planners*, London, RIBA Publishing, 2021, p 27.

21. National Building Specification (NBS), *What is BIM?*, https://www.thenbs.com/knowledge/what-is-building-information-modelling-bim (accessed 14 June 2023).

22. Royal Institute of Chartered Surveyors (RICS), *Certificate in BIM*, https://academy.rics.org/distance-learning/building-information-modelling-bim/certificate-bim-implementation-and-management (accessed 14 June 2023).

23. Royal Institute of British Architects (RIBA), *Understanding BIM: The past present and future*, https://www.ribabooks.com/Understanding-BIM-The-Past-Present-and-Future_9780367244187 (accessed 14 June 2023).

24. Royal Institute of British Architects (RIBA), *BIM Management Handbook*, https://www.ribabooks.com/BIM-Management-Handbook_9781859466056 (accessed 14 June 2023).

Image Credits

Figures 0.1, 1.4, 1.5, 1.12, 2.1, 2.11, 3.1, 3.8, 3.41 Authors; 1.0, 1.7, 1.8 Scott Brownrigg; 1.1 RIBA Collections; 1.2, 2.4 Pollard Thomas Edwards Architects; 1.3 Foster + Partners. Photo: Aaron Hargreaves; portrait James Aynsley / Ryder Architecture. Photo: Chris Lishman; 1.6 James Aynsley / Northumbria University; 1.9 Hawkins\Brown. Photo: Adrian Lambert; 1.10 Kirk McCormack; 1.11 RIBA Education and Learning. Photo: Jackie King Photographer; 1.13 Yavor Ivanov / London School of Architecture; 1.14 Laura Goodrick / RIBA Studio; 2.0 Ryder Architecture. Photo: Richard Lea-Hair; 2.2 Elliott Architects. Photo: Jill Tate; 2.3 Nelton Barbosa / London South Bank University; 2.5 Miles Brown / Northumbria University; 2.6 Timothy Austin Welch / RRA Architects; 2.7 Northumbria University. Photo: Jim Stephenson (clickclickjim.com); 2.8, 3.38a, 3.38b Bell Phillips Architects. Photo: Kilian O'Sullivan; 2.9, 3.2 Hawkins\Brown; 2.10 Anastasija Kostileva / London South Bank University; 2.12 Timothy Austin Welch / London South Bank University; 3.0, 3.5 Bowman Riley; 3.7 Authors / RIBA; 3.3 Ryan Bemrose / RIBA; 3.4 Kate Baker / RIBA; 3.6 RIBA North East Young Architectural Practitioners Forum; portrait Dieter Bentley-Gockmann / EPR Architects; 3.9 BDP; portrait Laura McClorey / FaulknerBrowns Architects; 3.10, 3.11 Laura McClorey / Northumbria University; portrait Jack Davies; 3.12 Jack Davies / University of West England (UWE Bristol); portrait Banah Rashid / Levitt Bernstein Architects; 3.13, 3.14 Levitt Bernstein; 3.15 Tom Stovold / Sheffield Hallam University; portrait Upinder Bahra / Hawkins\Brown; 3.16 Tom Spall Visuals / Hawkins\Brown; 3.17 Upinder Bahra / London South Bank University; portrait Jacinta Barham / FCBStudios; 3.18, 3.19 FCBStudios / University of Bristol; portrait Daniel Dyer / MawsonKerr Architects; 3.20 MawsonKerr Architects. Photo: Jill Tate; 3.21 Anna Dawson / Sheffield Hallam University; 3.22 Liam Whittingham / De Montfort University; 3.23a, 3.23b Mollie Lord / Lytle Associates Architects; portrait Daniel Kinghorn; portrait Sudhir Thumbarathy /Ryder Architecture. Photo: Chris Lishman; 3.24 NORR / PB Imagining / Newcastle University; portrait Stephen Smith / Wright & Wright Architects; 3.25 Wright & Wright Architects. Photo: Hufton+Crow; 3.26 Ashraf Salaman; 3.27a Emmanuel; 3.27b Wellcome Images; 3.28 Edited by Lee Marable, Text by Amy Sullivan, Illustrations by Erica Borgato; 3.29 Katie Shannon / Oxford Brookes University / FCBStudios; 3.30 Katie Shannon / Oxford Brookes University; portrait Katie Shannon / FCBStudios; 3.31, 4.0, 4.3 FCBStudios; portrait Sarah Nottet-Madsen / HTA Design LLP; portrait Delaram Nabidoost / HTA Design LLP; 3.32 HTA Design LLP; portrait Harbinder Birdi / Birdi and Partners; 3.33 Mehul Jethwa / DeMontfort University; 3.34 Laura McClorey / Northumbria University; 3.35a, 3.35b Chris Jenkins / Sheffield Hallam University; portrait, 3.36 Elizabeth Akamo / Scott Brownrigg; 3.37 Scott Brownrigg. Visualization courtesy of Studio Nesh; portrait Tim Bell, Melissa Dowler, Hari Phillips / Bell Phillips Architects. Photo: Kilian O'Sullivan; portrait, 3.39 Oliver Howard / London South Bank University; portrait Eleanor Lee / GSSArchitecture; 3.40 Eleanor Lee / University of Cambridge; 3.42 James Aynsley / Ryder Architecture / Northumbria University; 3.43 Rebecca Smith / xsite architecture LLP / Northumbria University; 3.44 Timothy Welch / RRA Architects / Atelier West; 3.45 Northumbria University. Photo: Mark Slater; 3.46 Harrison Lowthrop / Northumbria University; 4.1 Bell Phillips Architects; 4.2 Dean Ireland / Northumbria University; 4.4 Scott Brownrigg. Visualization courtesy of Wates; 4.5 LEAP: Lovingly Engineered Architectural Practice; 4.6 PH Partnership Architects; 4.7 MawsonKerr Architects; 4.8 HLM Architects. Sketch: Matthew Morrish; 4.9 Morris+Company

Index

Sponsors

Assael

Assael is an award-winning practice providing a cohesive suite of architecture, interior design, urban design, landscape architecture and design consultancy services. With nearly 30 years of experience, we have designed and delivered thousands of new homes for developers, investors, institutions and housing associations. These range from private-for-sale and private-for-rent, including 'Build to Rent', through to low-cost, shared-equity and affordable housing, as well as new models for housing, such as co-living and aspirational later living and intergenerational developments.

Foster + Partners

Foster + Partners is a global studio for sustainable architecture, urbanism, engineering and design, founded by Norman Foster in 1967. With offices across the world, the practice works as a single entity that is both ethnically and culturally diverse, with people central to all our endeavours.

HLM Architects have six studios across the UK, united through a one-team culture. Architecture, landscape and interior specialists with deep sector insight, the practice consistently innovates and seeks new ways to improve the design process. HLM's environmental and social objectives guide their approach to make better places for people. HLM were part of the Architectural Apprenticeship Trailblazer Group and are passionate about breaking down barriers and creating more accessible routes into our profession.

SPACE

SPACE Architects has over 60 years of experience designing buildings with a philosophy to impact people, places, and the planet positively. As a B Corp, the key to SPACE's identity is upholding ethical standards, building smarter, more efficient buildings, and forging strategic partnerships to drive the development of a built environment that benefits everyone.

FAULKNERBROWNS ARCHITECTS

FaulknerBrowns is a creative practice experienced in making buildings and places where people do better. From studios in Newcastle, Vancouver and Dublin, we use our experience to challenge what a particular building might look like, how it might be used, and the ways it can impact society. Our team of over one hundred talented architects, designers and technologists are also passionate about supporting architectural education, through mentorship and tutoring at schools and universities, and our vocal championing of architecture apprenticeships.

Hawkins\Brown

Hawkins\Brown is an architecture practice based in London, Manchester, Edinburgh, Dublin and Los Angeles. Founded more than 30 years ago and now run as an employee-owned trust, the firm brings a collaborative approach to projects across a range of types and scale in six main sectors: residential; education; workplace; healthcare; transport & infrastructure and civic, community & culture.

Ryder

Ryder are more than an architectural practice – we're a team of teams with diverse and extensive expertise. We lead projects in our unique integrated way, delivering exceptional value and a positive impact for our clients and communities. Founded in Newcastle upon Tyne in 1953, we now have teams collaborating across the UK and internationally, with a shared commitment to our ethos of Everything architecture – to improve the quality of the world around us and, in doing so, improve people's lives.